# Hell and After

LES MURRAY, born in 1938, grew up on a dairy farm at Bunyah on the north coast of New South Wales. Since 1971 he has made literature his full-time career. Carcanet publish his *Collected* and *Selected Poems* as well as his individual collections, including *Subhuman Redneck Poems* (1996, awarded the T.S. Eliot Prize), *Conscious and Verbal* (1999), *Poems the Size of Photographs* (2002); his essays and prose writings *The Paperbark Tree* (1992) and *Translations from the Natural World* (1993). His verse novel *Fredy Neptune* appeared in 1998 and won the Mondello Prize in Italy in 2004. His anthology of five earlier Australian poets from the 1920s to the 1960s, *Fivefathers*, was published in the Fyfield series in 1994. Les Murray received the Queen's Gold Medal for Poetry in 1999.

G000149857

Fyfield*Books* aim to make available some of the great classics of British and European literature in clear, affordable formats, and to restore often neglected writers to their place in literary tradition.

Fyfield*Books* take their name from the Fyfield elm in Matthew Arnold's 'Scholar Gypsy' and 'Thyrsis'. The tree stood not far from the village where the series was originally devised in 1971.

> *Roam on! The light we sought is shining still.*
> *Dost thou ask proof? Our tree yet crowns the hill,*
> *Our Scholar travels yet the loved hill-side*

from 'Thyrsis'

# Hell and After

*Four early English–language poets
of Australia*

Francis McNamara
Mary Gilmore
John Shaw Neilson
Lesbia Harford

Edited with introductions by
## LES MURRAY

CARCANET

First published in Great Britain in 2005 by
Carcanet Press Limited
Alliance House
Cross Street
Manchester M2 7AQ

in association with
ETT Imprint
59 Railway Street
Petersham NSW 2049
Australia

A CIP catalogue record for this book is available from the British Library

ISBN 1 85754 785 3

The publisher acknowledges financial assistance from Arts Council England

Typeset in Monotype Bembo by XL Publishing Services, Tiverton
Printed and bound in England by SRP Ltd, Exeter

# Contents

## *John Shaw Neilson*

## *Lesbia Harford*

# Introduction

Ten years ago. I published a book of selections from the work of five Australian poets (*Fivefathers*, Carcanet 1994) from the era of the 1930s to the 1960s, the period just before Australian literary studies became firmly established at home and abroad. These five, together with two or three others who already had collections in print in Britain, were the prime figures in the finest period our poetry has yet seen, and I wanted to display their work to readers abroad who had missed it in its time or later because of the insularity of older British Empire attitudes. Also, it was a gesture against the narrow national protectionisms which still impede much poetry in English from reaching its natural public across the whole Anglophone world. To complete this project, I have now made selections from four of the best Australian poets from before that magical era. These are pioneer voices, but of much more than merely historical interest. They come from the century and a half in which poetry began to be written in Australia, in English, and poets began to have names.

I have written elsewhere that for the first sixty or more thousand years of human culture in our country, poetry ruled everything; prose only arrived with the First Fleet in 1788. The sacred law of the Aboriginal people was deeply poetic in concept and expression. It was unwritten, and carried in the memory of initiated people down the generations. None of the myriad sacred songs of the land were attributed to known human authors. They were made by the ancestral creator spirits themselves, and formed part of the very body of such spirits, as did the natural sites in which the holy ones dwelt, the dances that honoured and expressed their stories, the paintings at the site and on participants' bodies, and even the devotees themselves during ceremonies. Incarnation is everywhere in Aboriginal religion, and it is by no means wholly a thing of the past. A lesser category of poetry, secular songs composed for enjoyment or comment, is still also practised wherever the tribal languages survive. It is usually known in Aboriginal English as 'rubbish' poetry or 'playabout' poetry, terms more affectionate and less derogatory than they sound. In line with the strict ban on naming the dead, at least for many years after they have passed on, most of these songs and their authors used to vanish from memory after a lifetime, but now some examples and their poets do get remembered, at least in Balanda (European) publications. *The Honey Ant Men's Love Song* edited by R.M.W. Dixon and Martin Duwell (University of Queensland Press 1990) is a particularly interesting sampler of such poetry, from groups all over Australia. Balanda readers will have realised that all Western poetry outside of holy scripture is 'rubbish' verse in Aboriginal terms. Sacred ritual texts can be sampled, but are best approached in standard books of reference in which the native material has been printed with the formal approval of tribal authorities. And even then it may not be intended for showing to uninitiated Aboriginal people, or to members of the opposite sex.

All Aboriginal poetry is sung; spoken verse arrived in Australia in 1788 along with the means of writing it down. For convicts, which is the term we use for victims of that strange marriage of hard Puritanism and early welfare, names were a fraught matter too, though in a different way. Many gave false names to the authorities every time they could, so as to confuse the records and maybe slip into a lesser category of punishment. Thus Francis McNamara sometimes appears in the records as Francis Goddard, and gets confused with a non-poet prisoner of that surname who had a different history. And then there is the famous Crow, or epigram of self-introduction, printed in this book, and its shorter ideogram form Frank the Poet, his claim on renown and on authorial credit. From his use of the term 'convict' – they preferred to call themselves 'prisoners' – we can tell that he meant his work to go beyond the penal barracks and reach the general public, which only knew the official term. Very little of it ever did so in his lifetime, though, and when the bits which emerged from the memory of fellow prisoners as relics of the penal period were collected, they were slow to be firmly attributed to their author – and it might have been much worse if he had not written out a holograph text for posterity.

The remaining three poets here were born in the second half of the nineteenth century, well after the convict era though within the old age of many who had suffered in it. Their use of names is essentially modern, though the two women poets still used their married surnames, as they would not do now. Patterns of publication were like those of today, except that more poetry was published in newspapers, with less of a class divide between vernacular balladry and more complex poetic forms. Class snobbery was provided then by exclusive schools which taught disdain of all 'colonial' art as against imported and Classical works. Then, as now, poetry depended on a self-selected small public of those who loved it, plus those they could recruit to their ranks. The first individual poetry collection in Australia, a book by Henry Kendall, was published in 1865, the year of Mary Gilmore's birth, and sold 3,000 copies. Readings as we know them would have been rare, but poetry would have been recited commonly at all sorts of social events, and a few colonial poets would have benefited from the custom of carrying books of verse on long journeys in the wilds because poetry was more succinct than prose and gave more mental nourishment per pound weight. All such books I've seen, though, were either Shakespeare or the Latin classics, plus one Scots Gaelic book. All three of our later poets here would have published in the defiantly Australian *Bulletin* weekly, more levelling than actually socialist; certainly John Shaw Neilson only rarely published anywhere else. The mystery, to me, of whether he might ever have heard the German *Lieder* which some of his poems resemble, is deepened by the fact that he would never normally have been invited to the refined soirées at which such music would be sung, and anyway he had no knowledge of German or other languages. Open concerts of good music would have been available to him only in Melbourne in the last years of his life. So the likeness I detect must be a parallelism of the sort common in art. By the time all three of my non-convict poets were at the height of their careers the great post-Tennyson slump in public acceptance of poetry would have been far advanced, with the stereotype of the alienated artist doing its work on artists and the wider community alike – just in time for the cinema to take the wider public away from us.

In the ten years since *Fivefathers*, penetration of the wider poetry market by Australians has increased to a degree. It's no longer all Les Murray, among non-expatriates. Now it's probably Les Murray plus John Kinsella, and that's all to the good! Not least because too much exposure abroad has long been a punishable offence in some circles at home. More overseas poetry, especially contemporary work, is available in Australian bookshops, and not all of it is now British, so colonial patterns of distribution are weakening. If the Australian–American Free Trade Agreement for which our country was dragged into the Iraq war passes our parliament and the American Congress, it will see a large increase in American books in our shops, which I applaud, though on top of the great damage to book buying done here by government refusal to exempt books from the GST (read VAT) when that came in six or seven years ago, poetry publishing in this country may disappear. The collapse of backlists and the refusal of most bookshops to carry titles for more than a year or so has had disastrous effects, as always suffered first by poetry, in its role as the mine-canary of culture. Moves are afoot to make the Internet the great centralised backlist for all poetry books, with provision for creating facsimiles of any which people want for their shelves. My suggestion was that such facsimiles be sold always at the price charged for them when they first came out. That would still give fair royalties to living writers and a marvellous advantage to the dead, who deserve any break they can get.

As in my earlier volume of epitomes, I have provided a brief, mainly bio-graphical introduction to each of the four poets here. I have kept to my rule of avoiding much critical discussion of their work, letting my judgement of each individual be shown by my selections. In the two cases where it·was relevant, I have mentioned the areas of their poeting which I passed over as less successful, but in all cases I have supplied a few details about the condi-tions under which they worked. Titles in square brackets are my additions to originally untitled poems.

Les Murray
Bunyah, NSW
March 2004

# Francis McNamara ('Frank the Poet')
## 1811–c. 1880

The first metropolis to be depicted in Australian literature was Hell. Before any terrestrial cities existed in Australia, the convict poet Francis McNamara describes a tour he was given through the infernal one. This jaunty Dantesquerie, dating from 1839, forms the high point of a set of poems that came out of a personal crisis in the last years of that decade. All are fresher, more varied and more adventurous than the Irish ballads he mainly created before and afterwards, though the latter can be very moving when sung according to contemporary tunes. They are often credited as the foundation of Australian bush balladry, which is still practised and loved in the bush, though its forms, its subjects and even its attitudes tend to be set in concrete.

Although McNamara always claimed to be a native of Cashel, in County Tipperary, at his trial in Kilkenny in 1832 for stealing a plaid he was described as coming from Wicklow. He was literate and had no previous convictions, but he drew seven years' transportation, and sailed from Cork on the *Eliza* on 10 May that same year. Arriving in Sydney in September, he would have gone straight to the large Hyde Park Barracks, which still exists under its later designation of the Mint in Macquarie Street. In his contemporary *Narrative of a Visit to the Australian Colonies*, James Backhouse reports that:

> One of the officers who had been there [at the Barracks] only about fifteen months, said, that upwards of one thousand men had been flogged in the course of that period. He stated his opinion to be, that how much soever men may dread flagellation, when they have not been subjected to it, they are generally degraded in their own esteem and become reckless after its infliction. This, we have found to be a very prevailing opinion in the Colony.

McNamara was flogged no less than fourteen times over the next eight years, receiving a total of six hundred and fifty lashes. His witty rebellious attitudes also brought him spells in solitary, three months on the treadmill and repeated bouts of hard labour on the gangs made to work in leg irons. It is a near miracle that his turning-the-tables poem 'A Convict's Tour to Hell' is so lightly done, free from sadism or rage.

By early 1838, McNamara had been assigned as a shepherd to the Scottish-owned Australian Agricultural Company, still remembered as the A.A. Co. This firm was set up in 1824 to cultivate the frontiers of settlement. The Peel River, on which the Country and Western music capital of Tamworth now stands, was then far out on the very edge, in Kamilaroi tribal country, but loneliness and the off-chance of a spear probably seemed a good bargain when compared with what the poet had endured. In October 1839, however, he was reassigned, to the Company's coal mines in Newcastle, where men worked naked underground in choking heat and lung-destroying dust. At this, he absconded, and was recaptured with a band of runaways, some of them carrying firearms. This could have got the whole party hanged, but milder counsels prevailed. Not much milder, in McNamara's case: he was sentenced to the awful Secondary Punishment Station at Port Arthur, in Van Diemen's Land, where the intent was to break the recalcitrant, not reform them. There, you could be flogged for not giving your towel to the laundry to be washed, or having a crust of bread in your clothes. Van Diemen's Land seems to have subdued the poet, though it didn't stop him making further rebel ballads for his mates to memorise and sing. Released in 1857, a year after the island colony's name was changed to Tasmania, the poet wandered back to New South Wales and thence into obscurity, with only odd sightings of him over the next two decades.

The curious gallimaufry of Irish stereotypes titled 'A Dialogue Between Two Hibernians in Botany Bay' was the only work by McNamara to appear in print in his lifetime, in the *Sydney Gazette* of 8 February 1840. Doubts have been expressed as to its authenticity, but some believe it is a set of coded messages for Whiteboys and Ribbon Men, members of Irish secret societies opposed to English rule and to the exactions of the Protestant Church of Ireland in the period after Catholic emancipation. McNamara may have been involved in this movement, and it is known that passwords in it were deliberately clownish and ridiculous. The rest of his work was carried in memory until 1861, when he wrote out the best of it in fine copperplate in a home-made book for the Calf family, of Windeyer near Mudgee. Some of his balladry was collected later in the nineteenth century as folk material, and only ascribed to him after careful detective work. McNamara may have been bilingual, and connected in some way with the McNamara bards of County Clare; he is clearly aware of Irish-language models and alludes to some of them, notably in the emblem of refusal in 'For the Company Underground'. He also seems to have admired Burns and Swift and Oliver Goldsmith, among English-language poets. His practice as a poet closely mirrors that of the hedge-poets of penal times, and he is the only poet whose work comes down to us from within the convict system as it existed in Australia, though its quality ranges far beyond the merely documentary.

# The Convict's Arrival

*Tune: 'Boolavogue'*

I am a native of the land of Erin,
And lately banished from that lovely shore,
I left behind my aged parents,
And the girl I adore.

In transit storms as I set sailing,
Like a bold mariner my coast did steer,
Sydney Harbour was my destination,
That cursed harbour at length drew near;
I then joined banquet in congratulation
On my safe arrival from the briny sea;
But alas! alas! I was mistaken –
Twelve years transported to Moreton Bay.

Early one morning as I carelessly wandered,
By the Brisbane waters I chanced to stray,
I saw a prisoner sadly bewailing,
While on the sunbeaming banks he lay.
He said, I have been a prisoner at Port MacQuarie,
At Norfolk Island and Emu Plain,
At Castle Hill and cursed Towngabbie –
And at all those places I've worked in chains.

But of all the places of condemnation,
In each penal station of New South Wales,
Moreton Bay I found no equal,
For excessive tyranny each day prevails.
Early in the morning as the day is dawning,
To trace from heaven the morning dew,
Up we are started at a moment's warning,
Our daily labour for to renew.

Our overseers and superintendents
All these cursed tyrants' language we must obey,
Or else at the triangles our flesh is mangled,
That is our wages at Moreton Bay.
For three long years I've been beastly treated;
Heavy irons each day I wore,
My poor back from flogging has been lacerated,
And oftimes painted with crimson gore.

FRANCIS MCNAMARA

Like the Egyptians or ancient Hebrews,
We were sorely oppressed by Logan's yoke,
Till kind providence came to our assistance
And gave this tyrant his fatal stroke.
Yes, he was hurried from that place of bondage
Where he thought he would gain renown,
But a native black, who lay in ambush,
Gave this monster his fatal wound.

Now that I've got once more to cross the ocean,
And leave this place called Moreton Bay,
Where many a man from downright starvation
Lies mouldering today beneath the clay.
Fellow prisoners be exhilarated,
And your former sufferings don't bear in mind,
For it's when from bondage you are extricated
We will leave those tyrants far, far behind.

## *Labouring with the Hoe*

I was convicted by the laws
Of England's hostile crown,
Conveyed across those swelling seas
In slavery's fetters bound.
For ever banished from that shore
Where love and friendship grow
That loss of freedom to deplore
And work the labouring hoe.

Despised, rejected and oppressed
In tattered rags I'm clad,
What anguish fills my aching breast
And almost drives me mad,
When I hear the settler's threatening voice
Say, 'Arise, to labour go;
Take scourging, convicts, for your choice
Or work the labouring hoe.'

Growing weary from compulsive toil
Beneath the noontide sun,
While drops of sweat bedew the soil
My task remains undone.
I'm flogged for wilful negligence
Or the tyrants call it so,
Ah, what a doleful recompense
For labouring with the hoe.

Behold yon lofty woodbine hills
Where the rose in the morning shines,
Those crystal brooks that do distil
And mingle through those vines –
There seems to me no pleasure gained,
They but augment my woe
Whilst here an outcast doomed to live
And work the labouring hoe.

You generous sons of Erin's isle
Whose heart for glory burns,
Pity a wretched exile who
His long-lost country mourns;
Restore me, Heaven to liberty
Whilst I lie here below
Untie that clue of bondage
And release me from the hoe.

# A Petition From the A.A. Co. Flocks at Peels River in Behalf of the Irish Bard

By permission of the great Esquire Hall
Being assembled here this day
Unanimously bleating all
For Him that's far away.

---

**Esquire Hall**: Charles Hall, stock superindentent of the Australian Agricultural Company from 1830, who resided at the A.A.'s Peel River estate from 1834.

Our noble sires in the rich vales
Of Germany long sported
But we alas to New South Wales
By the Company were imported.

We were bourne across the Main
From Holland and from Russia
Some from Saxony, more from Spain
France, Switzerland and Prussia.

We, the prime of the Company's stock
Fat wethers, rams and ewes
None excepted, all the flock
Peel for the Poet's woes.

Oft he has charmed with his notes
The Plains of fair Killala
To him we owe our fleecy coats
Our flesh, our hides, our tallow.

He ever proved our constant friend
'Tis plain from our contrition
In his behalf therefore we send
The following petition.

For years on the Poet's lawn we've grazed
And leaped o'er many a hurdle
To you our voices all are raised
Most noble Ebsworth of Burrell.

To honour thee we never cease
With reverence most profound
How much more Sire, when you release
The Poet from underground.

Each morning when the watchful cock
Announced the approach of day
At the folds he was seen with his flock
Before Sol's glittering ray.

**Killala**: properly Calala, the name of Hall's cottage at the Peel River.

**Ebsworth of Burrell**: James Ebsworth, superintendent of the A.A. Company 1838–9. Booral was the name of his residence near Strand.

HELL AND AFTER

The lofty wood crowned hills adorned
Were seen on the Plains
The truant like negligence he scorned
Of all the neighbouring swains.

By the fair Peel's evergreen side
We feasted every day
Our wants there amply were supplied
Whilst our Bard's merry lay

Joined with the notes of the sweet thrush
With melody filled the air
Birds to him flocked from every bush
So sweet his carols were.

Our tender lambs with him would play
And in his bosom lie
To Hawks they's often fall a prey
But for his watchful eye.

He reared them with a father's care
And fed the sickly ewes
Whilst other shepherds gambling were
On cards and dominoes.

Our wily foes, the native dogs
He chased for many a mile
Saint Patrick never drove the frogs
So swift from the Western Isle.

The King of Thessaly's numerous flocks
Once Telemachus kept
And from coverts and caverns in the rocks
Bears, lions and tigers crept.

To hear the music of his lute
But our Bard's plaintive songs
Not only charmed the senseless brute
But gathered the birds in throngs.

Far from the Peel's evergreen plains
In some wild lone retreat
In bitter and heartrending strains
We'll mourn our patron's fate.

Our cries from the hills shall resound
To the extremes of the Poles
If our friend goes underground
At Newcastle to wheel coals.

Why should the poet be sent down
To toil in a coal pit
Such service best suits a clown
But not a man of wit.

We yet shall hear his merry songs
On fair Killala's plain
Kind Heaven shall avenge the wrongs
Of our much injured swain.


# *[For the Company Underground]*

*Francis McNamara of Newcastle to J. Crosdale Esq. greeting*

When Christ from Heaven comes down straightway,
All His Father's laws to expound,
McNamara shall work that day
For the Company underground.

When the man in the moon to Moreton Bay
Is sent in shackles bound,
McNamara shall work that day
For the Company underground.

When the Cape of Good Hope to Twofold Bay
Comes for the change of a pound,
McNamara shall work that day
For the Company underground.

When cows in lieu of milk yield tea,
And all lost treasures are found,
McNamara shall work that day
For the Company underground.


**J. Crosdale**: William Croasdill, superintendent of the A.A. Co.'s Colliery
Establishment at Newcastle from 1837.

When the Australian Co.'s heaviest dray
Is drawn eighty miles by a hound,
McNamara shall work that day
For the Company underground.

When a frog, a caterpillar and a flea
Shall travel the globe all round,
McNamara shall work that day
For the Company underground.

When turkeycocks on Jew's harps play
And mountains dance at the sound,
McNamara shall work that day
For the Company underground.

When milestones go to church to pray
And whales are put in the Pound,
McNamara shall work that day
For the Company underground.

When Christmas falls on the 1st of May
And O'Connell's King of England crown'd.
McNamara shall work that day
For the Company underground.

When thieves ever robbing on the highway
For their sanctity are renowned,
McNamara shall work that day
For the Company underground.

When the quick and the dead shall stand in array
Cited at the trumpet's sound,
Even then, damn me if I'd work a day
For the Company underground.

Nor over ground.

**the Pound**: either a pen for strayed cattle or a sanctuary for escaped convicts. The canyon-like Burragorang Valley in the mountains west of Sydney was known to prisoners by this term.

# A Petition from the Chain Gang at Newcastle to Captain Furlong the Superintendent

*Praying Him to Dismiss a Scourger Named Duffy from the Cookhouse and Appoint a Man in his Room*

With reverence and submission due,
Kind sir those words are sent to you,
And with them a good wish too,
Long may you reign,
And like Wellington at Waterloo
Fresh laurels gain.

2nd
Your petitioners are under thy care,
In mercy therefore hear our prayer,
Nor let us wallow in despair,
But soothe each pang,
But allow no flogger to prepare
Food for your gang.

3rd
'Tis said that by your ordination
Our late cook lost his situation,
And Duffy is in nomination
His berth to fill;
But has not got our approbation,
Nor never will.

4th
Your judgement, Sire, put to good use,
Nor burthen us with foul abuse,
Full long we've drunk the dregs and juice
Of black despair,
Yet we can find another screw loose
Or two somewhere.

**Captain Furlong**: Captain Richard Tasker Furlong, superintendent of ironed gangs at Newcastle, January 1838 to February 1840.

**Duffy**: three convicts of this name were in the ironed gangs at Newcastle during the period 1837–8, but which of them was the flogger-cook is undetermined.

### 5th

Our jaws now daily will grow thinner,
And stomachs weak, as I'm a sinner,
For Duffy is a human skinner,
    Most barbarous wretch.
Each day I'd rather have my dinner
    Cooked by Jack Ketch.

### 6th

It matters not whether salt or fresh,
Even his touch would spoil each dish.
His cooking we never can relish –
    We'd rather starve.
For be assured 'tis human flesh
    He best can carve.

### 7th

To any rational being I appeal,
Whether he's fit to cook a meal
For a vile caterpillar or snail,
    Or a beast of prey.
Men he has scoured in every gaol
    In Botany Bay.

### 8th

I know the damned devils when they sit
To dine, will long for a savoury bit.
Now Duffy's just the person fit
    To boil their kettles,
To send him to the Bottomless Pit
    To cook their victuals.

### 9th

But did he even touch our meat,
A furnace our coppers wouldn't heat,
And every knife, fork, spoon and plate
    Would cry out Shame,
And in the midst of our debate
    Would curse thy name.

### 10th

Or if Saints Matthew, Mark, John and Luke,
With Moses who wrote the Pentateuch
Consented to make this flogger our cook.
     I'd say 'tis foul;
If I wouldn't swear it on the Book,
     Hell seize my soul.

### 11th

Now sir, your petitioners great and small
On bended knees before you fall;
Nor let us in vain for redress call,
     Drive Duffy away,
And as in duty bound we all
     Will ever pray.

'Tis needless to say the prayer was granted.

## A Convict's Tour to Hell

*Composed at Stroud A.A. Co. Establishment Station*
*New South Wales*

*Nor can the foremost of the sons of men*
*Escape my ribald and licentious pen.*
                    Swift

*Composed and written*
*October 23rd day, Anno 1839*

You prisoners of New South Wales,
Who frequent watchhouses and gaols
A story to you I will tell
'Tis of a convict's tour to hell.

Whose valour had for years been tried
On the highway before he died
At length he fell to death a prey
To him it proved a happy day
Downwards he bent his course I'm told
Like one destined for Satan's fold

And no refreshment would he take
'Till he approached the Stygian lake
A tent he then began to fix
Contiguous to the River Styx
Thinking that no one could molest him
He leaped when Charon thus addressed him
Stranger I say from whence art thou,
And thy own name, pray tell me now,
Kind sir I come from Sydney gaol
My name I don't mean to conceal
And since you seem anxious to know it
On earth I was called Frank the Poet.
Are you that person? Charon cried,
I'll carry you to the other side.
Five or sixpence I mostly charge
For the like passage in my barge
So stranger do not troubled be
For you shall have a passage free
Frank seeing no other succour nigh
With the invitation did comply
And having a fair wind and tide
They soon arrived at the other side
And leaving Charon at the ferry
Frank went in haste to Purgatory
And rapping loudly at the gate
Of Limbo, or the Middle State
Pope Pius the 7th soon appeared
With gown, beads, crucifix and beard
And gazing at the Poet the while
Accosts him in the following style
Stranger art thou a friend or foe
Your business here I fain would know
Quoth the Poet for Heaven I'm not fitted
And here I hope to be admitted
Pius rejoined, vain are your hopes
This place was made for Priests and Popes
'Tis a world of our own invention
But friend I've not the least intention
To admit such a foolish elf
Who scarce knows how to bless himself
Quoth Frank were you mad or insane
When first you made this world of pain?
For I can see nought but fire

A share of which I can't desire
Here I see weeping wailing gnashing
And torments of the newest fashion
Therefore I call you silly elf
Who made a rod to whip yourself
And may you like all honest neighbours
Enjoy the fruit of all your labours
Frank then bid the Pope farewell
And hurried to that place called Hell
And having found the gloomy gate
Frank rapped aloud to know his fate
He louder knocked and louder still
When the Devil came, pray what's your will?
Alas cried the Poet I've come to dwell
With you and share your fate in Hell
Says Satan that can't be, I'm sure
For I detest and hate the poor
And none shall in my kingdom stand
Except the grandees of the land.
But Frank I think you are going astray
For convicts never come this way
But soar to Heaven in droves and legions
A place so called in the upper regions
So Frank I think with an empty purse
You shall go further and fare worse
Well cried the Poet since 'tis so
One thing of you I'd like to know
As I'm at present in no hurry
Have you one here called Captain Murray?
Yes Murray is within this place
Would you said Satan see his face?
May God forbid that I should view him
For on board the *Phoenix* Hulk I knew him
Who is that Sir in yonder blaze
Who on fire and brimstone seems to graze?
'Tis Captain Logan of Moreton Bay
And Williams who was killed the other day
He was overseer at Grosse Farm
And done poor convicts no little harm
Cook who discovered New South Wales
And he that first invented gaols

Murray, Captain: superintendent of the *Phoenix* hulk and Governor of Carters Barracks.

Are both tied to a fiery stake
Which stands in yonder boiling lake
Hark do you hear this dreadful yelling
It issues from Doctor Wardell's dwelling
And all those fiery seats and chairs
Are fitted up for Dukes and Mayors
And nobles of Judicial orders
Barristers Lawyers and Recorders
Here I beheld legions of traitors
Hangmen gaolers and flagellators
Commandants, Constables and Spies
Informers and Overseers likewise
In flames of brimstone they were toiling
And lakes of sulphur round them boiling
Hell did resound with their fierce yelling
Alas how dismal was their dwelling
Then Major Morriset I espied
And Captain Cluney by his side
With a fiery belt they were lashed together
As tight as soles to upper leather
Their situation was most horrid
For they were tyrants down at the Norrid
Prostrate I beheld a petitioner
It was the Company's Commissioner
Satan said he my days are ended
For many years I've superintended
The An. Company's affairs
And I punctually paid all arrears
Sir should you doubt the hopping Colonel
At Carrington you'll find my journal
Legibly penned in black and white
To prove that my accounts were right
And since I've done your will on earth
I hope you'll put me in a berth

**Logan, Captain**: Commandant of Moreton Bay penal station, killed by Aborigines in 1830.

**Wardell, Dr Robert**: barrister, duelled with 'Hopping Colonel' Dumaresq, the Governor's private secretary – neither was wounded. Shot by absconding convicts in 1834.

**Morriset, Major**: superintendent of the dreaded Norfolk Island penal station in 1833.

**Cluney, Captain**: 17th Regiment, superintendent of Moreton Bay penal station from 1833.

Then I saw old Serjeant Flood
In Vulcan's hottest forge he stood
He gazed at me his eyes with ire
Appeared like burning coals of fire
In fiery garments he was arrayed
And like an Arabian horse he brayed
He on a bloody cutlass leaned
And to a lamp-post he was chained
He loudly called out for assistance
Or begged me to end his existence
Cheer up said I be not afraid
Remember No. 3 Stockade
In the course of time you may do well
If you behave yourself in Hell
Your heart on earth was fraught with malice
Which oft drove convicts to the gallows
But you'll now atone for all the blood
Of prisoners shed by Serjeant Flood.
Then I beheld that well known Trapman
The Police Runner called Izzy Chapman
Here he was standing on his head
In a river of melted boiling lead.
Alas he cried behold me stranger
I've captured many a bold bushranger
And for the same I'm suffering here
But lo, now yonder snakes draw near
On turning round I saw slow worms
And snakes of various kinds and forms
All entering at his mouth and nose
To devour his entrails as I suppose
Then turning round to go away
Bold Lucifer bade me to stay
Saying Frank by no means go man
Till you see your old friend Dr Bowman
'Yonder he tumbles groans and gnashes
He gave you many a thousand lashes
And for the same he does bewail
For Osker with an iron flail

**Flood, Sergeant**: 28th Regiment, at No. 3 Stockade in Newcastle, 1837.

**Chapman, Israel**: ex-convict, police informant and early Australian novelist.

**Dr Bowman**: arrived in New South Wales in 1798. Inspector General of Hospitals.

**Osker with an iron flail**: a hero in Irish saga literature.

HELL AND AFTER

Thrashes him well you may depend
And will till the world comes to an end
Just as I spoke a coach and four
Came in full post haste to the door
And about six feet of mortal sin
Without leave or licence trudged in
At his arrival three cheers were given
Which rent I'm sure the highest Heaven
And all the inhabitants of Hell
With one consent rang the great bell
Which never was heard to sound or ring
Since Judas sold our Heavenly King
Drums were beating flags were hoisting
There never before was such rejoicing
Dancing singing joy or mirth
In Heaven above or on the earth
Straightway to Lucifer I went
To know what these rejoicings meant
Of sense cried Lucifer I'm deprived
Since Governor Darling has arrived
With fire and brimstone I've ordained him
And Vulcan has already chained him
And I'm going to fix an abode
For Captain Rossi, he's on the road
Frank don't go 'till you see the novice
The magistrate from the Police Office
Oh said the Poet I'm satisfied
To hear that he is to be tied
And burned in this world of fire
I think 'tis high time to retire
And having travelled many days
O'er fiery hills and boiling seas
At length I found that happy place
Where all the woes of mortals cease
And rapping loudly at the wicket
Cried Peter, where's your certificate
Or if you have not one to show
Pray who in Heaven do you know?
Well I know Brave Donohue

**Rossi, Captain**: superintendent of the Police Office.

**Donohue, Jack** : bushranger shot by mounted police at Bringelly, NSW, in September 1830.

FRANCIS MCNAMARA

Young Troy and Jenkins too
And many others whom floggers mangled
And lastly were by Jack Ketch strangled
Peter, says Jesus, let Frank in
For he is thoroughly purged from sin
And although in convict's habit dressed
Here he shall be a welcome guest.
Isaiah go with him to Job
And put on him a scarlet robe
St Paul go to the flock straightway
And kill the fatted calf today
And go tell Abraham and Abel
In haste now to prepare the table
For we shall have a grand repast
Since Frank the Poet has come at last
Then came Moses and Elias
John the Baptist and Mathias
With many saints from foreign lands
And with the Poet they all join hands
Thro' Heaven's Concave their rejoicings rang
And hymns of praise to God they sang
And as they praised his glorious name
I woke and found 'twas but a dream.

# A Dialogue Between Two Hibernians in Botany Bay

Musha welcome to Botany, Paddy, my dear,
Yer the last man in Ireland, I thought of seeing here.
By my auntie Kate's side, you are my cousin jarmin,
And wid you I oft went to hear Father Mike's sarmin.

2nd
But how did this lagging of yours come to pass?
I'm inclined to think you neglected the mass.
And robbed your poor soul of felicity's joys,
By joining yourself to the cursed White Boys.

**Jenkins**: bushranger who shot Dr Wardell and was hanged for it in 1834. In his speech from the gallows he recommended the killing of tyrants at any opportunity.

### 3rd

The sea-sickness, Darby, has made me so weak,
That I'm hardly able at present to speak.
From wearing the darbies, my limbs are grown feeble,
And all the blame lies on the Man of the People.

### 4th

Cursed Daniel O'Connell, the great Agitator,
Is in my opinion a double-faced traitor,
From his seditious harangues had I kept away,
I ne'er should have visited Botany Bay.

### 5th

But tell me Darby, do you enjoy good health;
I heard when at home you possessed immense wealth.
'Twas the common conversation each night round the hearth,
That the Governor puts all his countrymen in berths.

### 6th

And they all flock around him like terrier dogs,
His first breath, like ourselves too, he drew in the bogs,
And the English assail him with vociferations,
For putting  his countrymen in situations.

### 7th

Places and offices of the greatest of trust,
But Darby, my friend, you know it is but just,
For never was a Paddy yet born of a mother,
That would not fight to death in defence of another.

### 8th

So we care not for Atheist, Jew, Christian or Turk,
So long as we're backed by our countryman Bourke,
Musha, Darby my friend, ain't the sea mighty deep,
Rather then be a sailor, I'd enlist for a sweep.

### 9th

For sweeps can repose on their soft sutty pillows
While mariners are tost up and down on the billows,
But if ever I return from cursed New South Wales,
I'll tell the ould people some wonderful tales.

FRANCIS MCNAMARA

## 10th

Describing the elements and waves in commotion,
And the curious animals I've seen in the ocean,
How black whales and sperm in droves gathered round us,
Spouting water on our decks, sufficient to drown us.

## 11th

How sharks followed after us like peelers and swaddies,
Anxiously awaiting to devour the dead bodies;
How the dolphin changes all colours when dying;
How I've seen lots of fish in the elements flying.

## 12th

Well I know they'll pitch myself to the dickens,
When I tell them about Mother Carey's fine chickens,
I'll tell the Mahers, Macnamaras, and M'Carty's,
All about iron gangs and road parties,

## 13th

How famous the hulk is for chaining and gagging,
How the penal men are used when doing their lagging,
I'll tell them about delegates, cooks, mates and victuallers
And give them a letter on Dungaree settlers.

## 14th

Now Darby since you're going to ould Ireland back,
Give my loving respects to my young brother Jack,
And pay the same tribute to Shamus my brother,
The same give to my affectionate mother.

## 15th

And don't forget to tell my dear daddy,
That I'm still his dutiful darling son Paddy,
And likewise Darby, tell my sister Onagh,
That I saw the big fish that swallowed up Jonah.

## 16th

Forget it not Darby, a fool can think of it,
Says you, it is the same beast, wolfed the poor prophet.
Give my love to my sweetheart Mary,
The star of Hibernia, the pride of Tipperary.

### 17th

Tell her that tho' twixt us there is a great barrier,
I may yet see the day that Pauddeen can marry her;
Yerra, well I know, that my neighbours and cousins,
Will all gather round you in scores and in dozens.

### 18th

And when you have told them all about lagging,
Musha Darby, tis yourself will get many a naggin.
Yerra then, Darby, you'll be in clover,
And when all the hugging and kissing is over,

### 19th

Stroll down to Maushe Connel, that lives in the moor,
And planted in the thatch, just over his door,
You'll find seven muskets and an old pike,
Deliver them yerself to ould Father Mike.

### 20th

To the right owners let his reverence return them,
If he refuses to do so, my honest friend, burn them.
Only for the muskets, well may I remark,
Poor Paddy today wouldn't be in Hyde Park.

### 21st

Tell the boys to beware of the great instigator,
Daniel O'Connell, the great agitator.
The poor Paddys can't comprehend what he's doing,
Damn him forever, 'twas he brought my ruin.

### 22nd

Tell the boys to desist from killing peelers and arson,
But cheerfully pay the tithe proctor and parson;
Why should they Darby, be left in the lurch,
You know they're the head of the Protestant Church.

### 23rd

To protect them, faith I'd spill my blood, every drop,
And not only the tenth, but the half of my crop,
I'd freely give them without hesitation,
To free me from Botany and vile transportation.

24th

I'd forsake the chapel and ould Father Mike,
The caravats, shilelagh and Ribbonman's pike;
I'd make peace with my God, live in charity with men,
Musha Darby, Botany Bay wouldn't catch Pat again.

## [Epigram of Introduction]

My name is Frank McNamara,
A native of Cashell, County Tipperary,
Sworn to be a tyrant's foe
And while I've life I'll crow.

## The Seizure of the Cyprus Brig in Recherche Bay, Aug. 1829

Come all you sons of freedom,
A chorus join with me,
I'll sing a song of heroes,
And glorious liberty
Some lads condemned from England
Sail'd to Van Diemens shore,
Their country, friends and parents,
Perhaps never to see more.

When landed in this colony
To different masters went,
For trifling offences
To Hobart Town gaol were sent.
A second sentence being incurr'd
We were ordered for to be
Sent to Macquarie Harbour,
That place of tyranny.

The hardships we'd to undergo,
Are matters of record,
But who believes the convict,
Or who regards his word?
For starv'd and flogg'd and punish'd,
Deprived of all redress,
The bush our only refuge,
With death to end distress.

Hundreds of us were shot down,
For daring to be free,
Numbers caught and banished,
To life-long slavery.
Brave Swallow, Watt and Davis
Were in our noble band,
Determ'd at the first slant,
To quit Van Diemens Land.

March'd down in chains and guarded,
On the *Cyprus* Brig conveyed,
The topsails being hoisted,
The anchor being weighed.
The wind it blew sou' sou' west
And on we went straightway,
Till we found ourselves windbound,
In gloomy Recherche Bay.

'Twas August eighteen twenty-nine,
With thirty-one on board,
Lieutenant Carew left the Brig,
And soon we passed the word.
The Doctor too was absent,
The soldiers off their guard,
A better opportunity
Could never have occurred.

Confin'd within a dismal hole,
We soon contrived a plan,
To capture now the *Cyprus*,
Or perish every man.
But thirteen turn'd fain-hearted
And begged to go ashore,
So eighteen boys rushed daring,
And took the brig and store.

We first address'd the soldiers,
'For liberty we crave,
Give up your arms this instant,
Or the sea will be your grave;
By tyranny we've been oppress'd,
By your colonial laws,
But we'll bid adieu to slavery,
Or die in freedom's cause.'

We next drove off the Skipper,
Who came to help his crew,
Then gave three cheers for liberty,
'Twas answered cheerly too.
We brought the sailors from below,
And row'd them to the land,
Likewise the wife and children
Of Carew in command.

Supplies of food and water,
We gave the vanquish'd crew,
Returning good for evil,
As we'd been taught to do.
We mounted guard with watch and ward,
Then hauled the boat aboard,
We elected William Swallow,
And obeyed our Captain's word.

The morn broke bright, the wind was fair,
We headed for the sea,
With one cheer more for those on shore
And glorious liberty.
For navigating smartly
Bill Swallow was the man,
Who laid a course out neatly,
To take us to Japan.

Then sound your golden trumpets.
Play on your tuneful notes,
The *Cyprus* Brig is sailing,
How proudly now she floats.
May fortune help the noble lads,
And keep them ever free,
From Gags, and Cats, and Chains and traps.
And cruel tyranny.

## [Epigram on Beef]

Oh Beef! Oh Beef! What brought you here?
You've roamed these hills for many a year.
You've felt the lash and sore abuse,
And now you're here for prisoners' use.


## Farewell to Tasmania

Farewell Tasmania's isle! I bid adieu
The possum and the kangaroo.
Farmers' Glory! Prisoners' Hell!
Land of Buggers! Fare ye well.

# Mary Gilmore
## 1865–1962

Child of a restless hero-father who filled her mind with ideas and old-world myths, Mary Gilmore grew up in the punctilio and social edginess of the years that were leading up to the emergence of the Anglophone world's first Labor Party in 1891. Born Mary Cameron near Goulburn in New South Wales, she was a child of the bush and never lost her love for its ways. Becoming a schoolteacher in the early 1890s she soon began to try her hand at writing the evocative 'Pars' (paragraphs) which were so popular in her time. She took part in union activities and in the founding of the Australian Labor Party, and remained one of its aristocracy all her life. In the early 1890s she followed the radical New Australia Movement in its utopian socialist venture to the wilds of Paraguay. There she married William Gilmore and went with him to Cosme when the initial settlement collapsed in dissention. The pair worked their passage back to Australia and farmed briefly at Casterton in western Victoria before separating permanently. Gilmore remains one of the very few Australian writers of her times to have a sense of Latin America; this comes out, however, in her prose rather than her poetry. Becoming a journalist, she founded and largely wrote the women's section of the *Australian Worker*, and gradually became a guru to hosts of people well beyond the Labor movement. Accepting the title of Dame of the British Empire in 1937 brought her little opprobrium even from ideologues, and by the 1950s she could write a column, often the same column, in both the *Catholic Weekly* and the Communist *Tribune*. She had become a national institution, and her youthful face now appears on the Australian ten dollar note. The literary note.

Coming from before modernism, she disliked everything about it and learned little from it; this would estrange her from literary interests that became dominant in her later life. There is an experimental impulse in her, though, as attested by the wide range of styles and moods in her writing. Much of her verse is marred by lingering Victorian diction, and her dialect writing in Scots and Irish accents, to which she was drawn by her Ulster background and the prevalence of Scots and Irish immigrants in her day, never escaped from a fatal staginess. It is sad that all of her poems on Aboriginal themes seem to be led by their very sympathy to an orotund diction which smothers them; she never matched the lapidary remark of one Wiradgery tribesperson to whom she had shown some European portraits: 'these are pictures of clothes, not of people!' License to write in clear current idiom came to her from popular and newspaper verse, as can be seen from the social observation she first employed it on. The selection of her work I have made here is a fairly strict one, but that is the sort of selection time imposes on all poets. At her best, she wrote a handful of our very finest poems.

In her lifetime, Gilmore was much loved for her recollections of colonial life, which always conveyed the real other-worldliness of an age both recent and utterly different in spirit. Averaging two or three pages in length, these often have the beauty and concentration of prose poems. As do many of her notes and prefaces to poems; I have included a couple of these to give the flavour of her reminiscent writings without seeming to make up weight with the longer ones. She did occasionally heighten her memories a little. This even gave her the seed of a striking poem in this selection, 'Fourteen Men', which describes with curious aplomb her seeing fourteen Chinese gold diggers hanged as part of the Lambing Flat race riots, outside a town later called Young in New South Wales. In fact, no Chinese were hanged there, and the riots ended four years before she was born. But who would deny fiction to a poet? As a much-belated world première, this selection also includes a poem, 'Judged', which I found by chance in a bunch of Gilmore typescripts mis-filed in another author's manuscript box in the Public Library of New South Wales. It does not appear in any of her published collections, and to my knowledge has never previously been published at all.

# When Myall Creek Was New

The Ellighans boasted of high descent,
　　They had pedigree long as your leg;
But they lived in a hut that hadn't a fence,
　　And the latch of the door was a peg.
The Ellighans' name was Allingham-Flint;
　　But the bush is a law to itself,
And a slip of the tongue, and a new name comes.
　　And the old is laid on the shelf.

When the harvesters came 'twas 'Hurry up, quick!'
　　With brownies and billies of tea;
The sugar was brown and the tea was black,
　　But that didn't matter to me!
Your arms might crack and your back might break,
　　And the stubble might prickle your legs,
But billies went up, and billies went down,
　　And the brownie was 'currants and eggs!'

The harvesters went to the Ellighans, too,
　　But the harvesters liked us best,
And when I have mentioned a reason or so
　　You'll never be asking the rest!
For, Salt in the cooking, Mixture for cakes,
　　Or Batter for Puff-da-lunes,
*They* tasted *theirs* with a lick o' the point –
　　But *we* always tasted with spoons!

The Ellighan hands were thick like a spud,
　　Their feet were heavy as spades,
In spite of an ancestry ever so long,
　　Asleep in Plantagenet glades;
And the Ellighan ways were never our ways,
　　They sniffed as they passed us by
With a pedigreed shout, as the distance grew,
　　Of 'Irish' and 'pigs' and 'stye!'

MARY GILMORE

Gone are the years, and Grandmother's voice,
 And her 'Never you mind nor heed:
'Tis the dead must often turn them about
 To wonder what of the breed!'
And memory plays like a harp in the wind
 A thin and an olden tune:
'They tasted theirs with a lick of the point,
 But Grandmother asked for a spoon!'


## *I Am the Idle*

I am the idle, bone-idle I lie,
Under the lift where the white clouds fly.

A rose nid-nods, and the grass bows low,
Each kissed by the winds that vagrant blow.

Cicadas are scraping a riddle of song,
A path-finder ant goes hasting along;

Through tussock and fern the brown beetles creep –
I turn me about like a dog, and sleep.


## *Eva Has Gone*

The women they tell how it all began,
And the men that her face was sunny.
Eva has gone with the sailor-man;
She has taken the ready money.

She said 'I am off in a leaky boat;
What a fool was I to marry!
But the ten-pound note and the five-pound note
Are easy enough to carry.'

Her husband toiled as a slow man can
To put those notes together.
He had stuck to his work when many a man
Would never have faced the weather.

The sailor-man he was six foot high
And of the salt sea smelling.
On earth or in hell there was never a lie
That he was not proud of telling.

Some dark things out on the line she hung;
'Twas a fine warm day for drying.
Oh, cruel was she, for her child was young,
And the neighbours found it crying.

The women said as they gathered near
And nodded one to the other,
'Her child she has left, and God can hear
A child when it has no mother.'

'Now,' they said, 'she has lost her all;
Not even her God can pity.'
And they heavily talked of her dreadful fall
And her open shame in the city.

'She might have gone by the night,' said they,
'When the lovers creep together.
'Twas a shameful way that she went by day,
Like a wild thing off the tether.'

The women they speak of her laziness,
And the men that her mouth was honey.
Eva has gone with a sailor-man;
She has taken the ready money.

The women they say that her eyes were hard,
The men that her mouth was pretty;
And some will say they have gone to the Bush,
And some say into the City.

Her husband said as he worked one day
With his old mate in the quarry,
'The women, they make the worst of it;
And the sailor will soon be sorry.'

## Eternal Claim

He hath kissed me and burned me, he with his mouth;
Hath sucked up my life and parched me with his drouth;
Hath smitten me and stricken me and left me in the field:
– And yet, if he came again, what could I do but yield?

He called me from Eternity for his father-hood of life;
He called to me eternally for mothering of life;
He found me and bound me – who left me in the field:
– O God, if he came again, what could I do but yield?

## The Linen for Pillow…

I had a lover,
   He loveth me not,
His way he went
   And me forgot;
Yet may his sleep
   Be soother and sound
As though he had never
   Dealt me a wound.

I had a lover
   And oh, he was false
Though I had set him
   Over all else!
Yet may his meat
   Ever be sweet,
The rough o' the road
   Soft to his feet.

He hath forgot me,
   Passing me over
Like a lone blossom
   Nipped in the clover;
Yet must I wish him,
   Though deep is my woe,
The Linen for pillow
   Wherever he go.

# Judged

*'She didn't seem a bit sorry that the baby was dead, in fact, she seemed rather glad.'*

Extract from a letter

It pined, and pined, and cried,
    And I had not the time
    To tend it, either night
Or day, and so it died.

But once, before it went,
    It looked at me, and smiled,
    A little, fleeting smile,
So pitiful, so spent.

I could have cried aloud;
    But who would care? Who help?
    Who grieve because of one
Small soul lost in the crowd?

And, late, as night wore through,
    It gasped, and sighed. – And I –
    I know that I was glad
When it passed out... O, you

Who guiltless hold yourselves,
    Give ear! When women work
    All day, and half the night,
And starve, and sell themselves

For bread; they do not weep
    Because the children die,
    They only weep because
The children live.

MARY GILMORE

## The Rue Tree

The Rue Tree is the tallest tree,
    None other is so tall;
The Rue Tree is the smallest tree,
    None other is so small;
But O, where'er its dark head grows,
    One root is in the heart,
And every man its sad fruit knows,
    Or walks as one apart.

There was a Rue Tree had no leaf
    But a cross-piece set above;
On either hand there hung a thief,
    But at its heart was Love;
And judges walked behind a Rue
    That grew a gallows-tree,
Where they who followed after knew
    Whose breath came piteously.

And many a one in prison cell
    Waters a Rue Tree there,
As down his slow tears dropping well,
    And his sighs break on air.
For the Rue Tree is the tallest tree,
    None other is so tall;
The Rue Tree is the smallest tree,
    O none so sad and small.

## These?

Are these our people's leaders? These
Whose babbling voices
Sound in familiar keys,
Like farm-yard noises?
The world churns like a maggot-pit,
Turmoiled in strife,
While the mice-minded sit,
Nibbling at life.

# In Poverty and Toil

## I. Anger

Git up an' out, you lazy lump,
  I'll give y' late a-bed! –
The fire to make, the cows to milk,
  The chickens to be fed;

The children waiting to be dressed,
  The table to be laid;
The floor to sweep, the beds to air,
  The breakfast to be made;

The bread to mix, the clothes to sort,
  The churn to scald and scour –
An' I've to come an' call you,
  Though it's daylight near an hour!

## II. Contrition

Be up an' out of bed, my girl,
 As quick as you can be;
There ain't no morning rest, my girl,
 For such as you an' me.

It's workin' early, workin' late,
 Year in, year out, the same;
Until we seem but work-machines,
 An' women but in name.

Life grinds the sweetness out of us,
 Life makes us hard an' cold;
We kiss shame-faced, an' grow uncouth;
 Unlovely – young and old.

Kind speaking dies for lack of use,
 Soft ways mean only grief;
And in the lash of biting words
 We find a half relief.

So up, and out to work, my girl,
    We have no time to waste,
Our lot, the bitter bread of life,
    We eat in bitter haste.


# The Truest Mate

I don't know whether 'tis well to love,
    Or whether 'tis well to hate,
But I know this well, that the man who has sinned
    Is ever the truest mate.

For the man who has sinned his sins himself,
    And learned what a man may learn,
Is wiser than he who has lived untried
    By the fires that make, or burn.

He knows the needs of the human heart,
    The want in another's will,
And sees excuse where the untried man
    Sees only the love of ill.

He sees the good, and he sees the bad,
    And judges these two between,
And he knows the thing that counts for most.
    Is seldom the thing that's seen.

For one may know what a man has done,
    But who, how a man has tried?
And who shall say if a man go straight
    For purity's sake, or pride?

And who shall say if a sinner sin
    For love of the sin or no;
Or whether he drift in ignorance
    Of the things that a man should know?

I don't know whether 'tis well to love,
    Or whether 'tis well to hate,
But I know this well, that the man who has sinned
    Is ever the truest mate.

As late as the 1870s, where there was a family the clothes-lines were put up behind the kitchen, and no male visitor, coming or going, ever rode or drove round that way. I remember Mrs John Stinson, of Kindra Station, with a voice of outrage telling her husband that she would never have a certain young man at the house again, as he had committed the unpardonable sin of riding past the clothes-lines, when the washing had not yet been brought in.

The rule was to hang sheets, towels, tablecloths and napery on the first line near the kitchen, especially where there was a man cook, whether white or Chinese. The feminine wear, protected by this, went on the next or middle line, and the 'coloureds' and boys' wear on the third or back line. Thus the middle line was shielded from sight. No man who knew manners ever rode by those lines.

The blacks had similar taboos. Whenever they camped, the women's side of the place was forbidden to the men. If a man trespassed he could be banished or killed as a breaker of tribal law.

Father once ordered a man off the station he managed because he had ridden into a camp on the women's side, quite regardless of their feelings. 'Only that the blacks know me,' father furiously said, 'you might have had us all killed!'

## The Forest Prayed

The forest prayed,
All night it prayed for rain;
By day it bowed its head;
Its prayer was vain.

The sun went down,
And, as up-spanned the moon,
Again was heard that sad
And broken rune.

Night-long it pled
In murmurous refrain;
The sun rose up red-eyed;
There came no rain.

Through the long days,
The leaves, where nothing stirred,
Hung like the feathers of
A wounded bird.

# The Coming

Once I came as a ghost,
I came lighter than air
From my shadowy coast,
And none saw me there.

But somebody said,
'It is cold, and the fire
Has gone low, poke the bed
Of the log; send the flame higher!'

Why did I come? I knew
Not of whence or of where,
Nor the door I came through,
Or why I was there.
Only I knew
That I came.


# Outcast

Something came walking, last night,
    Round the house and round;
It had no face that one could see,
    And its voice had no sound.

Pity reached out to it there,
    But, however pity tried,
It was too lost for pity,
    The thing outside.

# All Souls

*For Walter Stone*

Unlatch the door
And let them in;
Evil is done,
No more they sin.

They are the lost,
Even as Christ,
When, desert-held,
He kept a tryst.

Pull down the blind,
Lay out the food,
Where, by the hearth,
Of old they stood.

Set wide the door,
Then come not near;
God is their Awe,
But man their fear.

Based on an old Gaelic story, and told by my father.


# Heritage

Not of ourselves are we free,
Not of ourselves are we strong;
The fruit is never the tree,
Nor the singer the song.

Out of temptation old, so old
The story hides in the Dark Untold,
In some far, dim, ancestral hour
There is our root of power.


MARY GILMORE

39

The strength we give is the strength we make;
And the strength we have is the strength we take,
Given us down from the long-gone years,
Cleansed in the salt of others' tears.

The fruit is never the tree,
Nor the singer the song;
Not of ourselves are we free,
Not of ourselves are we strong.

## Awakened

His eyes looked into mine,
    (O, look that made me wise!)
I hid my own, although
    My world lay in his eyes.

I turned away my face,
    My breath came like a sob;
And to his heart my own
    Gave answer, throb for throb.

I could not raise my eyes,
    Lest he should read therein;
And trembled, woman-wise,
    And woman-waked, within.

## The Kiss

Lean over the fence and kiss? Not I!
    If the tide leapt up to a kiss
    The fence were a bar too low,
Or the kiss was a lie!
    And a kiss that's a lie is none
    When everything's said and done.

Lean over the fence and kiss?
　　Philander and play the fool?
Blood that is blood is hotter than this.
　　Or life were easy to school!

Lean over the fence and kiss? I? Never!
　　Scorn to your Safe-to-lean-over,
　　Half-and-half lover!
Give me the kiss that is all —
Or nothing forever.


## The Babe

Kisses on the dimpled arm?
　　On the mouth of red;
Kisses on the throat and chin,
　　On the silky head.
Let me have him, no one near,
　　Naked in my arms;
Let me kiss, with none to see,
　　Wrists and rosy palms.
Leave him just a little while,
　　Leave us all alone —
Never at my breast will lie,
　　Children of my own.


## Fourteen Men

Fourteen men,
And each hung down
Straight as a log
From his toes to his crown.

Fourteen men,
Chinamen they were,
Hanging on the trees
In their pig-tailed hair.

Honest poor men,
But the diggers said 'Nay!'
So they strung them all up
On a fine summer's day.

There they were hanging
As we drove by,
Grown-ups on the front seat,
On the back seat I.

That was Lambing Flat,
And still I can see
The straight up and down
Of each on his tree.


## The Tenancy

I shall go as my father went,
A thousand plans in his mind,
With something still held unspent,
When death let fall the blind.

I shall go as my mother went,
The ink still wet on the line;
I shall pay no rust as rent,
For the house that is mine.


## Of Certain Critics

They say, as though they sorrowed,
I have borrowed;
Yet, for all their grieving pains,
One proud certainty remains –
Never from these little gifted
Critics have I lifted!

# The Gift

Tortured, tormented, and enslaved,
    A prisoner love made of me,
    Who, as a wild bird, once was free;
But from the heart's death me he saved.


# Never Admit the Pain

Never admit the pain,
    Bury it deep;
Only the weak complain,
    Complaint is cheap.

Cover thy wound, fold down
    Its curtained place;
Silence is still a crown,
    Courage a grace.


# The Harvesters

In from the fields they come
To stand about the well, and, drinking, say,
'The tin gives taste!' taking in turn
The dipper from each other's hands,
The dregs out-flung as each one finishes;
Then as the water in the oil-drum bucket lowers,
They tip that out, to draw a fresher, cooler draught.
And as the windlass slowly turns they talk of other days,
Of quaichs and noggins made of oak; of oak
Grown black with age, and on through generations
And old houses handed down to children's children,
Till at last, in scattered families, they are lost to ken.
'Yet even so the dipper tastes the best!' they say.
Then having drunk, and sluiced their hands and faces,
Talk veers to fields and folk in childhood known,
And names are heard of men and women long since dead,
Or gone because the spirit of adventure
Lured them from familiar scenes to strange and far.

Of these old names, some will have been so long unheard
Not all remember them. And yet a word its vision brings,
And memory, wakened and eager, lifts anew
The fallen thread, until it seems the past is all about them
Where they group, and in two worlds they stand –
A world that was, a world in making now.

Then in a sudden hush the voices cease,
The supper horn blows clear, and, from community
Where all were one, each man withdraws his mind
As men will drop a rope in haulage held,
And, individuals in a sea of time,
In separateness they turn, and to the cook-house go.


## The Saturday Tub

Dreaming I sat by the fire last night,
And all at once I jumped in a fright,
For I really thought, as the embers burned,
That somehow or other the years had turned,
And I was back where I used to be,
In eighteen hundred and something three,
Still in my place for the old bath tub,
Flannel and soap, and rub-a-dub-dub!

All in a line by the fire we stood –
'Johnny, keep still!' and, 'Hughie, be good!'
And as, one by one, we took it in turn
To stand in a tub the size of a churn,
It was, 'Where's the flannel?' and, 'Mind the soap!'
Slither and slide, and scuffle and grope,
Soap and flannel, and rub-a-dub-dub,
Each in his turn in the old bath tub!

On Saturday nights we stood in a row,
Spotlessly clean and white as the snow,
Except that the little round knees stayed brown,
Though the soap had smothered us toes to crown;
The firelight flickered on breast and brow
(I loved it then, and I love it now!)
Lathered and flannelled, scrub-a-dub-dub,
Each in his turn from the old bath tub!

When each little shirt went over each head,
'Gentle Jesus' and 'Our Father' said,
It was 'Quick with a kiss!' and 'Now then, run!
And off into bed with you, every one!'
Ah, would we had kept, in these later days,
To the kind old path and the simple ways,
When nation by nation, rub–a–dub–dub,
The world fell into a blood–bath tub!

## Bones in a Pot

Little Billy Button
Said he wanted mutton;
Miss Betty Bligh
Said she wanted pie;
But young Johnny Jones
Said he wanted Bones –
Bones in a pot,
  All hot!

## Old Botany Bay

I'm old
Botany Bay;
Stiff in the joints,
Little to say.

I am he
Who paved the way,
That you might walk
At your ease to-day;

I was the conscript
Sent to hell
To make in the desert
The living well;

I bore the heat,
I blazed the track –
Furrowed and bloody
Upon my back.

I split the rock;
I felled the tree:
The nation *was* –
Because of me!

*Old Botany Bay*
*Taking the sun*
*From day to day...*
*Shame on the mouth*
*That would deny*
*The knotted hands*
*That set us high!*

The kangaroos were patriarchal. They lived in family groups, though they fed in hundreds (and at times in thousands) on the plains and among the trees of the forests. I do not remember them ever bedding-down in the open, but always under or near trees, the 'Old Man,' as the blacks named him, standing sentinel to the last. I have never seen an Old Man kangaroo remove sticks before lying down; perhaps his weight made it unnecessary; or perhaps, like a man, he slept heavily and did not feel them, while the does, like women, slept lightly because of the young. But the does invariably lifted with their delicate 'hands' even small twigs, and tossed them away before lying down. If they felt one left under them, they would get up and look for it, throwing it away when it was found.,

HELL AND AFTER

## The Little Shoes that Died

These are the little shoes that died.
  We could not keep her still,
But all day long her busy feet
  Danced to her eager will.

Leaving the body's loving warmth,
  The spirit ran outside;
Then from the shoes they slipped her feet,
  And the little shoes died.


## Eve-Song

I span and Eve span
A thread to bind the heart of man;
But the heart of man was a wandering thing
That came and went with little to bring:
Nothing he minded what we made
As here he loitered, and there he stayed.

I span and Eve span
A thread to bind the heart of man;
But the more we span the more we found
It wasn't his heart but ours we bound!
For children gathered about our knees:
The thread was a chain that stole our ease.
And one of us learned in our children's eyes
That more than man was love and prize.
But deep in the heart of one of us lay
A root of loss and hidden dismay.

He said he was strong. He had no strength
But that which comes of breadth and length.
He said he was fond. But his fondness proved
The flame of an hour when he was moved.
He said he was true. His truth was but
A door that winds could open and shut.

And yet, and yet, as he came back,
Wandering in from the outward track,
We held our arms, and gave him our breast
As a pillowing place for his head to rest.
I span and Eve span,
A thread to bind the heart of man!

## The Road

The road broke under the wheels,
And a new rut made a new road;
The mare's foal ran at her heels –
The quick when her pulse had slowed;
Seed in the furrow knew Spring,
And, high in the air, the wing
Of a gull soared upward going: –
And suddenly I was immortal,
Knowing the old beauty of death!

## Somehow We Missed Each Other

Somehow we missed each other,
Passed each other by unknowing;
I who sought you, you who sought me,
With hearts that throbbed for hopes and fears:
Passed each other in the early going,
Missed each other in the early years.

Somehow we missed each other,
We two poor bankrupt souls, sowing
A harvest that we recked not of;
Now others' sorrows claim our tears,
Others call us in our later going,
Others hold us in our later years.

# Second-hand Beds

When snuggled up warm in your quilts of down,
    Has it ever entered your heads
To think of the people who live down town,
    And sleep in their second-hand beds?
Your blankets are clean, and your sheets are white,
    They are changed whenever you choose,
But how would you feel if your lot each night
    Was a bed that looked like a bruise?

You sit on a chair to take off your boots,
    Your room has a wardrobe and table,
A drawer for studs, and a place for suits,
    And quiet to sleep – if you're able!
But how would you like it when bedtime came
    To have but a threadbare blanket,
Glad it were only a blanket in name,
    And you, as you turn, out-flank it?

Has it ever come into your well-kept heads,
    As you lie in your quilts of down,
To think of the women in second-hand beds
    At the other end of the town?
Have you ever watched, on Saturday night,
    The poor, with their fingered shillings,
Hang over the spreads that never were white,
    And feel at the ticks for fillings?

Have you ever thought of the babies born,
    Who have never once lain on sheets,
Brought up and bred to the marriage-morn
    On the filth of second-hand streets?
Had you ever wanted for half a crown,
    Or slept like a cat on the leads,
You'd ache for the women, outed and down,
    Who sleep in their second-hand beds!

## Famous

He sat, a leader and acclaimed by men,
    And all his heart was with the yellow corn;
He saw the paddocks of his youth again,
    And weathered hut where he and his were born.

And as he dreamed he heard the wind
    Blow up and down the tawny wheat,
And marked the rustle, how it fell and thinned.
    And died upon the wind in its retreat.

He heard the milkers lowing at the rails,
    And saw his father rise and let them in;
Caught the horn's rattle on the closing bails,
    Heard the first milking on the pail strike thin.

The firelight leaped behind his chiselled brass,
    A bell beside his polished table rang;
He heard a troop of horses pass,
    The battered door of an old stable clang.

Upon the wall the great companioned him:
    His heart was with a little barefoot lad,
Running to find a ferny brookside dim,
    And chequered waters by a forest pad.

## Nationality

I have grown past hate and bitterness,
I see the world as one;
But though I can no longer hate,
My son is still my son.

All men at God's round table sit,
And all men must be fed;
But this loaf in my hand,
This loaf is my son's bread.

The pine-tree is a king,
He lifts high his steeple;
But greater is the wheat –
The wheat is a people.

# In Wesleyan Days, Wagga Wagga

When service was held at full of the moon,
And old Brother Uncles gave out the tune,
In the slab-walled meeting-house long, long ago
The dimity hoods sat all in a row,
And as line by line of the hymn was read
They followed and sang as the leader led

By a rag-wick light (they were Wesleyans then),
They gathered together, women and men
And little they cared for the world outside,
It's grasping for riches, its pomp and pride,
For their hearts were full and their voices glad
As they praised the Lord, whatever they had.

There were Withers, and Biddle, and Whittell and Clode –
Hales, Dowlings, and Johnstons, from Brucedale Road –
And they muddled up hymns that they started too high
(Which, later, Miss Wagg sent up to the sky),
Till Beattie came in with his fine baritone,
And Heydon stood up, a basso alone!

And the 'sittings' were stools, in that year of grace,
'Family' – 'Single' – according to place;
And, fashioned at home by primitive art,
Each 'head' brought his own on shoulder or cart,
And many a child on a cushion sat,
Brought in from the gig, and thankful for that.

I remember on tins they sat, at a pinch
With the young girls crowded up, inch by inch;
And the tins brought biscuits, and butter and eggs
To fatten the minister's children's legs;
While the boys (now grey heads) stood back at the wall,
And at Amen time groaned loudest of all.

And my youngest uncle he stood with them there,
While the A-a-amens he said would have raised your hair
And my youngest aunt, in a white sun bonnet
Kept well at the back (she'd a bow pinned on it)
For bows on bonnets were never allowed
Lest the spirit of woman should grow too proud.

Ah well, and ah well! it is long ago, now,
And Time has furrowed us all with his plough;
But I still remember the threats and the storms
When the 'stoolers' came in and 'collared the forms';
For, when forms were 'bread' and stools were a 'stone',
Then even piety asked for its own.

The stools were of slab and had auger-hole legs
Where the ends stuck up through the tops like pegs,
And no one in sermon time sat upon these
But looked on a form as elegant ease;
For the forms were sawn, and levelled, and planed,
And your back, if it ached, was All that pained.

I was only a child, but I loved the way
That the sun through a crack sent down his ray,
Or the nights when the moon rode clear and bright
And a beam shot in of silvery white;
Sometimes a knot-hole would act as a funnel
And show us a ray like a ghostly tunnel.

A slush-lamp at first by the 'pulpit' stood,
Which Biddle would trim till the light was good,
Till my grandmother brought a brass candlestick
And a home-made candle that bent on its wick;
And then at a meeting held late 'twas decided
That four tin sconces should be provided.

When the sconces came and the strings were untied,
But three were all that the town could provide,
For never a viaduct, then, nor a rail
Reached out of the town for the Sydney trail;
And a month it took till the teams came back
When macadam was wanting to cover the track.

There was hardly a dwelling in Johnston Street
When the old-time Wesleyans used to meet,
And even Fitzmaurice Street still showed bark,
And had ruts that might have swallowed the Ark
Had Wagga been known the time of the Flood,
With its long roads buried in flats of mud.

But sunlight or moonlight, or cloudy and dark,
On a track no more than a shadowy mark,
They came and they offered their souls to God,
Who whispered His name as they ploughed the sod;
Then the Sabbath Day was His holy day,
And never a man was ashamed to pray.

Ah me, and ah me! it is all in the past,
With the moonlight 'feast' and the monthly 'fast',
With the day we forgot and had meat for dinner,
And nobody spoke, each felt such a sinner;
And lest such a scandal should happen again,
We marked the fasts with a red ink pen!

Now the 'chapel' is 'church,' with stalls for a choir,
And the once long sermon is short – 'by desire';
But I often dream that the kind old ghosts
Must gather together in shadowy hosts
Withers and Uncles, and Whittell and Biddle,
Our chairs at the side, the stools in the middle.

And I like to think that the hymns that they chose
From their shadows arise as of old they rose;
That the earnest prayer and the penitent form
Still take the Kingdom of Heaven by storm;
Baldwins, and Elliotts, and Beatties in front
With the boys at the back to heel up the hunt.

O neighborly hands and neighborly hearts
How memory burns and the hot tear starts!
For, shades in the moonlight, I see you pass
Where the white of the frost is crimping the grass,
And I hear you sing, when the nights are dark,
Where you set your course to an heavenly mark.
O brave forerunners, who never sought fame,
How the church you loved must treasure each name!

# The Road to Gunning

May the divil's foot be on them that emptied from the land
The little farms and homesteads we had on every hand,
The places where the children came in tribes across the floor,
And watching out, 'till father comes,' stood mother at the door!

The divil's cure be on the crew that let the roof-tree rot
That lasted where the child outgrew the measure of his cot,
That saw the first young fruit-tree set, and watched the orchard bloom,
Ere money turned men off the land to give the sheep more room.

And may his mark be on the hand that let the sliprails out,
Where bright as butterflies at play the children ran about;
Where once grew cabbages in rows, and peas in summer green,
And now but beaten tracks of hoofs and rabbit-hills are seen.


# Verdicts

### 'Angry Penguins'

You who have moved so long
In a contorted world of form,
For whom no single chord
Can bring a tuneful song,
Who, in some dark land of Heth,
Storm and Chimera ask,
How will your hearts endure
The simpleness of death?


### Some Modernists

Eyes fixed they sit and stare –
Brooders, not even dreamers –
Seeking to bring gold from a shadow,
And fruit from a passing wind.
'Ours are the mountains of thought,' they cry,
'In us dwells the all–comprehending mind!'
But only their own kind talk to them.
Or use their idiom.

## The Road

He who rides the ass of faith
Rides in easy travel;
He who walks on his two feet
Finds the road is gravel.


## The Thumb

'Intellect' said one, 'is the world's builder!'
But from the prehistoric and the dumb
Came this: 'Not intellect, but memory!'
And, lifting up its thumb,
It said: 'The first remembered movement made by this
Was man's first step towards the skies.'

# John Shaw Neilson
## 1872–1942

As the son of often-destitute small farmers, 'Jock' Neilson was obliged during most of his life to support himself and his relations by backbreaking work as a road mender, ditch digger, quarryman and itinerant farm labourer. He has been called a rare example, in modern times, of a genuine 'primitive' poet of quality. He has been compared with Burns, Clare and W.H. Davies, and was probably even further outside the world of literature than they were. From his childhood, Neilson had only some scraps of remembered Burns and Hood, some Coleridge and Fitzgerald's *Rubaiyat*. He also had the words of some older Scots and Irish songs and a great love of Stephen Foster's melodies, but as an invaluable background to these few influences he had his feckless father's great love of poetry; the elder Neilson wrote verse copiously and even published some of it in the newspapers. The idea of a literary vocation was thus natural to his son; if his admired father was for it, who could be against it?

Conditions for a worker poet in backblocks Victoria were harsh enough, but Neilson's only recorded complaints were against his weak eyesight. By the age of thirty, this congenital defect had cut him off altogether from reading, and he had gone from writing out his poems in large letters on big sheets of butcher's wrapping paper to relying on relatives and workmates to act as his amanuenses. Some of his labourer scribes were known to exclaim 'Jesus!' at what they were asked to write down line by line, and the manuscripts Neilson sent to his editor and mentor in Sydney often bore original spellings and punctuation. The mentor was A.G. Stephens, literary editor of the seminal *Bulletin* newspaper; his advocacy on Neilson's behalf was invaluable and lasted over forty years. Less valuable were some aspects of his editing, correcting non-existent errors and encouraging the poet in his worst habits of archaism and sentimentality. The two only ever met once, on a trip to Sydney in 1926.

Poverty and shyness are adduced as the reasons for his never having married, and he is reported never to have had any close relationships, but what he did not choose to reveal need not be inferred. Like others of his family, he suffered a number of nervous breakdowns. Some of these have been related to deaths in his family, others to crises of religious belief. Neilson appears to have been haunted by the severe punitive imagery of his mother's strict Scottish Presbyterianism – one of his escapes from that is detailed in the poem 'The Gentle Water Bird', which he dedicated to Dame Mary Gilmore, and mystical rebuttals of Calvinism can be found everywhere in his work. In 1928, when his health was breaking down, a job was found for him as a messenger with a government department in Melbourne. Neilson's poetry has been widely and increasingly admired in Australia in the years since his death, and its musical lyricism has been praised in the highest terms. Quite often, it has qualities of the German *Lieder* he had probably never heard of. It seems strange that little of it has ever been set to music. Fewer people have praised his delicate humour and his love of justice, evinced especially in poems such as 'Take Down the Fiddle, Karl', in defence of innocent German residents of Australia during the First World War.

# The Crane is My Neighbour

The bird is my neighbour, a whimsical fellow and dim;
There is in the lake a nobility falling on him.

The bird is a noble, he turns to the sky for a theme,
And the ripples are thoughts coming out to the edge of a dream.

The bird is both ancient and excellent, sober and wise,
But he never could spend all the love that is sent for his eyes.

He bleats no instruction, he is not an arrogant drummer;
His gown is simplicity – blue as the smoke of the summer.

How patient he is as he puts out his wings for the blue!
His eyes are as old as the twilight, and calm as the dew.

The bird is my neighbour, he leaves not a claim for a sigh,
He moves as the guest of the sunlight – he roams in the sky.

The bird is a noble, he turns to the sky for a theme,
And the ripples are thoughts coming out to the edge of a dream.


# The Gentle Water Bird

*For Mary Gilmore*

In the far days, when every day was long,
Fear was upon me and the fear was strong,
Ere I had learned the recompense of song.

In the dim days I trembled, for I knew
God was above me, always frowning through,
And God was terrible and thunder-blue.

Creeds the discoloured awed my opening mind,
Perils, perplexities – what could I find? –
All the old terror waiting on mankind.

Even the gentle flowers of white and cream,
The rainbow with its treasury of dream,
Trembled because of God's ungracious scheme.

And in the night the many stars would say
Dark things unaltered in the light of day:
Fear was upon me even in my play.

There was a lake I loved in gentle rain:
One day there fell a bird, a courtly crane:
Wisely he walked, as one who knows of pain.

Gracious he was and lofty as a king:
Silent he was, and yet he seemed to sing
Always of little children and the Spring.

God? Did he know him? It was far he flew...
God was not terrible and thunder-blue:
– It was a gentle water bird I knew.

Pity was in him for the weak and strong,
All who have suffered when the days were long,
And he was deep and gentle as a song.

As a calm soldier in a cloak of grey
He did commune with me for many a day
Till the dark fear was lifted far away.

Sober-apparelled, yet he caught the glow:
Always of Heaven would he speak, and low,
And he did tell me where the wishes go.

Kinsfolk of his it was who long before
Came from the mist (and no one knows the shore)
Came with the little children to the door.

Was he less wise than those birds long ago
Who flew from God (He surely willed it so)
Bearing great happiness to all below?

Long have I learned that all his speech was true;
I cannot reason it – how far he flew –
God is not terrible nor thunder-blue.

Sometimes, when watching in the white sunshine,
Someone approaches – I can half define
All the calm beauty of that friend of mine.

Nothing of hatred will about him cling:
Silent – how silent – but his heart will sing
Always of little children and the Spring.


## *The Flautist*

He may know too much
Of where life began.
I will not speak; he is
Too hazy a man.

I saw with music
The speech of his pride,
I saw him put tears on
The face of a bride.

I heard him playing,
As a bold man plays
For a sweetheart's journey
On holidays.

But he made sorrow
Outside all sound,
For a dead man creeping
To the underground.

He knows too much
Of where Death began,
I will speak no more with
This hazy man.

## To a Runaway Sound

Nay, but I love you not. Who set you free?
From what mad prison came you to hasten the cool heart of me?

Go away out then, where lovers would sweeten the ground;
No law will heed you, for you are a runaway sound.

You would have angels to listen where thought cannot climb.
Fall away over white dresses in holiday time.

Did you lie deep in a forest or down in dark sea?
For all your light step you call up slow things to me.

Go away out of the colours, rattle the ground,
But stoop not my dull heart to hasten, you runaway sound.

## For the Little Boys Out of Heaven

On the serene day, first of the seven,
I ache for innocence: I walk to hear
The little boys who have come out of Heaven.

I was as one entombed in a bright dwelling.
There were angelic flavours that did hover;
Only of joy they told, and still were telling

'Twas sundown, and the bells came in at seven.
Sweet were the foreheads, sweet the unwavering eyes.
I saw the boys who had come out of Heaven.

Listening I say, they have defeated sorrow
With a new beauty round about them dreaming
Hastening or evil will not come tomorrow.

Lustre of women is around them falling
As a remembrance of unearthly meadows,
While from their lips the heavenly thoughts are calling.

They have not fear; the bells they are at seven.
Peace did they bring with all flowers of the meadow.
Calm are the boys who have come out of Heaven.

# The Ballad of Remembrance

I met a man out Bathurst way in the middle of the year,
He had an honest, kindly face and eyes without a fear;
A pleasant man to look upon and a pleasant man to hear.

And he would talk as men will talk of what their hands have done,
Of plains and hills and the wilderness where sheep and cattle run,
Of the bitterness of frost and rain and the blinding of the sun.

He had the bushman's ready eye, and he heard the faintest sound,
The names he knew of all that flew, or ran upon the ground,
His knowledge was not of the kind that is with scholars found.

One thing I saw whene'er I talked of all red history,
Of England's victories on the land, her strength upon the sea,
He listened quietly, but would say no generous word to me.

The silence of the man was such, that I would more and more
Speak of the English; there had lived never on earth before
A race so just and merciful, – his silence made me sore.

One night I spoke of English law, and what the English do –
'Listen,' he said, 'and I will tell a shameful thing to you,
'Twas old when I was born, this night it comes up ever new.

'Too long have I been in the bush, my thinking may be slow,
But when you praise the English, then knowing all I know,
If I did not speak, then I should feel the lowest of the low.

'My father, he could fight, although he was but bone and skin,
I saw him fight with a big man, who had the heavy chin,
And the heavy fist. I stood two hours and saw my father win.

'My father had the slow speech, and his words came tenderly;
When we were splitting in the bush one day we took a tree
With young birds in the nest, all day he could not speak to me.

'An open-handed man he was, as all who knew him tell;
He was not hard in anything, he strove to teach us well;
He said, "There's something in a man, that they dare not buy or sell."

'My father could not read or write – now little children can, –
Of Death, and things at the back of it, his simple reasoning ran,
And he said, "I can't believe that God is bitter like a man."

'How quiet he was, because he stared they said his eyes were dim,
But when he drank, those eyes would change, and his jaws would be so grim,
And the thoughts at the bottom of his heart came tumbling out of him.

'"Some things there are," my father said, "I keep remembering,
A man's body is coarse, he said, though he may be a king,
But the body of a sweet woman, that is the holy thing."

\* \* \*

'"Twas in your England that he starved and he would not dare to kill,
He knew the law, and the law it said, his mouth he must not fill.
All Wisdom came from God, he heard, and the hunger was His Will.

'There was the food before his eyes, and why should he be bound?
The rich men owned each inch of earth and the riches underground;
They would have owned the soul of man had such a thing been found.'

'These laws,' I said, 'were harsh, but they have long since disappeared,
Wherever strong men live and thrive, is English law revered,
That flag is loved, and we are proud to know that it is feared.'

But the man he said, 'You boast that all the English laws are fair,
Long have I heard such tales, they seem like dust upon the air,
For the English sent my father here for the shooting of a hare.

'One day we were in the deep bush, my father's tongue was free,
I was not far into my 'teens and his back he showed to me,
And even now when I think of it, my eyes can scarcely see.'

'These laws,' I said, 'were cruel laws, they were in every land,
The English gave you all you have and you fail to understand
That laws are made for the English, by the people's own command.'

The man he said, 'I may be dull, you speak of English law,
Would you so love it had you seen the shameful thing I saw?
For me that back is always bare, those wounds are always raw.

'He was a convict forced to work, when the squatter ruled the land,
For some slight fault his master put a letter in his hand
And he said, "Take this to Bathurst Gaol, they'll make you understand."

'Too well the law, my father knew, the law of Lash and Chain,
That day he walked to Bathurst Gaol, 'twas in the blinding rain,
And they flogged his flesh into his bones – then he walked back again.'

The man he said, 'I have always heard that English laws are fair,
We are a part of England, and her fighting glory share,
But the English sent my father here for the shooting of a hare.

'My father was of England and it is against my will,
Of any nation on the earth, to speak one word of ill;
But I know the English by one mark – my eyes can see it still.'

Then spoke I still of England, I would not lightly yield,
'England,' I said, 'is strong, she does the little nations shield,'
And the man he said, 'Some things there are that never can be healed.'

## *The Poor, Poor Country*

Oh 'twas a poor country, in Autumn it was bare,
The only green was the cutting grass and the sheep found little there.
Oh, the thin wheat and the brown oats were never two foot high,
But down in the poor country no pauper was I.

My wealth it was the glow that lives forever in the young,
'Twas on the brown water, in the green leaves it hung.
The blue cranes fed their young all day – how far in a tall tree!
And the poor, poor country made no pauper of me.

I waded out to the swan's nest, – at night I heard them sing,
I stood amazed at the Pelican, and crowned him for a king;
I saw the black duck in the reeds, and the spoonbill on the sky,
And in that poor country no pauper was I.

The mountain-ducks down in the dark made many a hollow sound,
I saw in sleep the Bunyip creep from the waters underground.
I found the plovers' island home, and they fought right valiantly.
Poor was the country, but it made no pauper of me.

My riches all went into dreams that never yet came home,
They touched upon the wild cherries and the slabs of honeycomb,
They were not of the desolate brood that men can sell or buy,
Down in that poor country no pauper was I.

*　*　*

The New Year came with heat and thirst and the little lakes were low,
The blue cranes were my nearest friends and I mourned to see them go;
I watched their wings so long until I only saw the sky,
Down in that poor country no pauper was I.

## The Lad Who Started Out

October and the shining air put wondrous thoughts in him;
And he could fight and climb and ride, and he could shoot and swim:
The baby was about him yet, but a mystic fever ran
In the little lad who started out one day to be a man.

Tempting and fair, two furlongs off, there rose the forest green
Where the subtle bees had hid their home; but the river ran between.
Out of a gaudy dandelion a whispering pirate flew,
And the fever spoke in the dear lad and told him what to do.

Ay, 'twas a madness of the heart! but of the kind that goes
With the kingly men and conquerors, wherever red blood shows:
A thousand fathers stormed in him and drove him in his dream;
Quickly he cast his clothes aside and walked into the stream.

The babe's blue was on his eye, and the yellow on his hair:
Proudly he held the good broad chin that all the heroes bear:
But oh! too high and far and strong the snow-fed river ran
For the little lad who started out one day to be a man.

*　*　*

Ah, madly comes the taste of him in coats the children wear,
And the red caps of the toddlers, and ruddy legs and bare:
The pirates whispering in the gold say grievous things of him,
And the leaves along the sunshine laugh, because he could not swim.

There is a woman sweet and kind, a woman calm and grey,
And her eyes have love for little lads in all their boisterous play.
She says, 'So was his merry heart! so was his pretty chin!
My sorrow must run out and out, for I dare not keep it in.'

But when the snow-fed waters come, and the yellow's in the air,
She looks not long on the blue sky; for his blue eyes are there:
Oh, the yellow had not left his head when all her tears began
For the little lad who started out one day to be a man.


# The Child Being There

She will be looking at all the bright shops in the town,
Some like the sunrise, and some like the sun going down:
– 'Such lights,' she says, 'are in Heaven. Oh, that I might stare
Right in through the door into Heaven! – my child being there.'

She being so long a great sinner – ill-spoken – unwise –
Softly she goes now, and looking at God with both eyes;
And she will say at the midnight – her heart lying bare –
'Surely I have part of Heaven? – my child being there.'

Loneliness hangs on her dress – it is now the long worn:
On the shoes that are broken – the hat that has fallen forlorn:
She says: 'Would God see me, I wonder now? if I should stare
Right in through the door into Heaven – my child being there.'

She will be looking at women the young and the strong,
And the frocks of the little ones laughing and dancing along:
''Tis hard that they have all the riches!' she says in despair:
'I helped in the making of Heaven – my child being there.'

Poor though her body be, still it is goaded of Love:
– This that can hasten the tiger, and moan with the dove:
This that can make God a shadow. She says: 'I will dare!
I will look for a moment in Heaven! – my Child being there.'

# Love in Absence

When thou art gone but a little way
    I am in a cold fear:
The day like a long sickness is,
    And I count the moon a year.

When thou art gone but a little way
    I am in a deep alarm:
I cry, Oh God! her dear body,
    If it should come to harm!

When thou art gone and light is gone
    I fiercely wish thee near:
The day like a long sickness is,
    And I count the moon a year.

Now mournfully I dream I fall
    Where uncouth shadows be:
I foot it on the mist, – the heart
    Renounces liberty.


# The Hour of the Parting

Shall we assault the pain
    It is the time to part
Let us of Love again
    Eat the impatient heart.

There is a gulf behind
    Dull voice and fallen lip,
The blue smoke of the mind,
    The grey light on the ship.:

Parting is of the cold
    That stills the loving breath,
Dimly we taste the old
    The pitiless meal of Death.

# Love's Coming

Quietly as rosebuds
  Talk to the thin air,
Love came so lightly
  I knew not he was there.

Quietly as lovers
  Creep at the middle moon,
Softly as players tremble
  In the tears of a tune;

Quietly as lilies
  Their faint vows declare
Came the shy pilgrim:
  I knew not he was there.

Quietly as tears fall
  On a wild sin,
Softly as griefs call
  In a violin;

Without hail or tempest,
  Blue sword or flame,
Love came so lightly
  I knew not that he came.


# To a Lodging-House Canary

In you are all the good jigs of the Irishman out for a day,
Little one! close to the Maker you whistle away.

Prisoned, and born in a prison, and yet in your song
Out to the top o' the twilight you take us along.

The goodman has need of sweet noises; he calls to his dame:
And she, being barren, she knows but the edge of the flame.

You dance into heaven, O rude one! – and higher and higher
You mock at the craven who eats not his fill o' the fire.

Free men we are not: we cannot come out of the fear.
Call the dead! Let the dead march in your merriment here!

Soldier you are, and good neighbour: you come not to cry
Of any dull ache in the body or doubt in the sky.

In you are all the good jigs of old Irishmen out for a day,
Little one! close to the Maker you whistle away.


## The Sweetening of the Year

When old birds strangely-hearted strive to sing
and young birds face the Great Adventuring:

When manna from the Heaven-appointed trees
bids us to banquet on divinities:

When water-birds, half-fearing each blue thing,
trace the blue heavens for the roving Spring:

When school-girls listening hope and listening fear:
They call that time the sweetening of the year.

\* \* \*

When schoolboys build great navies in the skies
and a rebellion burns the butterflies:

Sunlight has strange conspiracies above
and the whole Earth is leaning out to Love:

When joys long dead climb out upon a tear:
They call that time the sweetening of the year.


## A Limerick

A charming young lady named Brewster
Trimmed her hat with the head of a rooster.
    When they asked 'Can it crow?'
    She smiled and said 'No –
It can't do that now but it used to.'

# The Soldier is Home

Weary is he, and sick of the sorrow of war,
   Hating the shriek of loud music, the beat of the drum;
Is this the shadow called glory men sell themselves for?
    The pangs in his heart they have paled him and stricken him dumb!
        Oh! yes, the soldier is home!

Still does he think of one morning, the march and the sun!
   A smoke, and a scream, and the dark, and next to his mind
Comes the time of his torment, when all the red fighting was done!
   And he mourned for the good legs he left in the desert behind.
        Oh! yes, the soldier is home!

He was caught with the valour of music, the glory of kings,
   The diplomats' delicate lying, the cheers of a crowd,
And now does he hate the dull tempest, the shrill vapourings –
   He who was proud, and no beggar now waits for his shroud!
        Oh! yes, the soldier is home!

Now shall he sit in the dark, his world shall be fearfully small –
   He shall sit with old people, and pray and praise God for fine weather;
Only at times shall he move for a glimpse away over the wall,
   Where the men and the women who make up the world are striving
                      together!
        Oh! yes, the soldier is home!

Simple, salt tears, full often will redden his eyes;
   No one shall hear what he hears, or see what he sees
He shall be mocked by a flower, and the flush of the skies!
   He shall behold the kissing of sweethearts – close by him, here, under
                      the trees –
        Oh! yes, the soldier is home!

# Stony Town

If ever I go to Stony Town, I'll go as to a fair,
With bells and men and a dance-girl with the heat-wave in her hair:
I'll ask the birds that live on the road; for I dream (though it may not be)
That the eldest song was a forest thought and the singer was a tree.

Oh, Stony Town is a hard town! It buys and sells and buys:
It will not pity the plights of youth or any love in the eyes:
No curve they follow in Stony Town; but the straight line and the square:
– And the girl shall dance them a royal dance, like a blue wren at his prayer.

Oh, Stony Town is a hard town! It sells and buys and sells:
– Merry men three I will take with me, and seven and twenty bells:
The bells will laugh and the men will laugh, and the girl shall shine so fair
With the scent of love and cinnamon dust shaken out of her hair.

Her skirts shall be of the gossamer, full thirty inches high;
And her lips shall move as the flowers move to see the winds go by:
The men will laugh, and the bells will laugh, to find the world so young;
And the girl shall go as a velvet bird, with a quick step on her tongue.

She shall cry aloud that a million moons for a lover is not long,
And her mouth shall be as the green honey in the honey-eater's song:
If ever I go to Stony Town, I'll go as to a fair,
And the girl shall shake with the cinnamon and the heat-wave in her hair.


# Stephen Foster

*Composer of 'My Old Kentucky Home'*

Who was the man? he was not great or wise,
　　He lived in sore distress,
Always he went with pity in the eyes
　　For burnt-out Happiness.

He who was poor had melodies of gold,
　　He had the rude man's Art,
No one can now deny him – he could hold
　　The quick roads to the heart.

## Tell Summer that I Died

When he was old and thin
And knew not night or day,
He would sit up to say
Something of fire within.
How woefully his chin
Moved slowly as he tried
Some lusty word to say:
Tell Summer that I died.

When gladness sweeps the land,
And to the white sky
Cool butterflies go by,
And sheep in shadow stand;
When Love, the old command,
Turns every hate aside,
In the unstinted days
Tell Summer that I died.

## The Hen in the Bushes

Call me the man seeing
    Too much in air:
Low by the little hen
    Love it is there.

Winds of the Summer,
    The red, the unkind,
Tilt at her motherhood
    Resolute, blind.

As a Queen guarding
    Her jewels so rare,
Patiently all the day
    I see her there.

'Tis the Old Tyrant
    To her body come,
He who will leave us all
    Weighted and dumb.

He the Old Tyrant
   Will many men slay,
He will most gladly
   Burn women away.

He turns the peasant lad
   To the raw soil,
He calls by candle-light
   Slaves to their toil.

He it is urging up
   Cities of sighs;
Who has seen Pity yet
   Enter his eyes?

He it is under
   The war and the moan,
He it is under
   The lies on the stone.

Soon will the thin mother
   With her brood walk;
Keen is the crow – and keen,
   Keen is the hawk.

Call me the man seeing
   Too much in air...
Low by the little hen
   Love it is there.

# The Moon Was Seven Days Down

'Peter!' she said, 'the clock has struck
　　At one and two and three;
You sleep so sound, and the lonesome hours
　　They seem so black to me.
I suffered long, and I suffered sore:
　　– What else can I think upon?
I fear no evil; but, oh! – the moon!
　　She is seven days gone.'


'Peter!' she said, 'the night is long:
　　The hours will not go by:
The moon is calm, but she meets her death
　　Bitter as women die.
I think too much of the flowers. I dreamed
　　I walked in a wedding gown,
Or was it a shroud? The moon! the moon!
　　She is seven days down.'


'Woman!' he said, 'my ears could stand
　　Much noise when I was young;
But year by year you have wearied me:
　　Can you never stop your tongue?
Here am I, with my broken rest,
　　To be up at the break of day:
– So much to do; and the sheep not shorn,
　　And the lambs not yet away.'


'Peter!' she said, 'your tongue is rude;
　　You have ever spoken so:
My aches and ills, they trouble you not
　　This many a year, I know:
You talk of your lambs and sheep and wool
　　– 'Tis all that you think upon:
I fear no evil; but, oh! the moon!
　　She is seven days gone.'

'Peter!' she said, 'the children went:
    My children would not stay:
By the hard word and the hard work
    You have driven them far away.
I suffered, back in the ten years
    That I never saw a town:
– Oh! the moon is over her full glory!
    She is seven days down!'

'Woman!' he said, 'I want my rest.
    'Tis the worst time of the year:
The weeds are thick in the top fallow,
    And the hay will soon be here.
A man is a man, and a child a child:
    From a daughter or a son
Or a man or woman I want no talk
    For anything I have done.'

'Peter!' she said, ''Twas told to me,
    Long back, in a happy year,
That I should die in the turning time
    When the wheat was in the ear;
That I should go in a plain coffin
    And lie in a plain gown
When the moon had taken her full glory
    And was seven days down.'

Peter, he rose and lit the lamp
    At the first touch of the day:
His mind was full of the top fallow,
    And the ripening of the hay.
He said, 'She sleeps,' – but the second look
    He knew how the dead can stare:
And there came a dance of last beauty
    That none of the living share.

How cool and straight and steady he was:
 He said, 'She seems so young!
Her face is fine – it was always fine –
 But, oh, by God! her tongue!
She always thought as the children thought
 Her mind was made for a town.'
– And the moon was out in the pale sky:
 She was seven days down.

He sauntered out to the neighbour's place
 As the daylight came in clear:
'The wheat,' he said, 'it is filling well,'
 And he stopped at a heavy ear.
He said, 'A good strong plain coffin
 Is the one I am thinking on.'
– And the moon was over his shoulder:
 She was seven days gone.


## Schoolgirls Hastening

Fear it has faded and the night:
 The bells all peal the hour of nine:
The schoolgirls hastening through the light
 Touch the unknowable Divine.

What leavening in my heart would bide!
 Full dreams a thousand deep are there:
All luminants succumb beside
 The unbound melody of hair.

Joy the long timorous takes the flute:
 Valiant with colour songs are born:
Love the impatient absolute
 Lives as a Saviour in the morn.

Get thou behind me Shadow-Death!
 Oh ye Eternities delay!
Morning is with me and the breath
 Of schoolgirls hastening down the way.

# The Orange Tree

The young girl stood beside me. I
    Saw not what her young eyes could see:
— A light, she said, not of the sky
    Lives somewhere in the Orange Tree.

— Is it, I said, of east or west?
    The heartbeat of a luminous boy
Who with his faltering flute confessed
    Only the edges of his joy?

Was he, I said, borne to the blue
    In a mad escapade of Spring
Ere he could make a fond adieu
    To his love in the blossoming?

— Listen! the young girl said. There calls
    No voice, no music beats on me;
But it is almost sound: it falls
    This evening on the Orange Tree.

— Does he, I said, so fear the Spring
    Ere the white sap too far can climb?
See in the full gold evening
    All happenings of the olden time?

Is he so goaded by the green?
    Does the compulsion of the dew
Make him unknowable but keen
    Asking with beauty of the blue?

— Listen! the young girl said. For all
    Your hapless talk you fail to see
There is a light, a step, a call,
    This evening on the Orange Tree.

— Is it, I said, a waste of love
    Imperishably old in pain,
Moving as an affrighted dove
    Under the sunlight or the rain?

Is it a fluttering heart that gave
    Too willingly and was reviled?
Is it the stammering at a grave,
    The last word of a little child?

– Silence! the young girl said. Oh, why,
    Why will you talk to weary me?
Plague me no longer now, for I
    Am listening like the Orange Tree.


## In the Dim Counties

In the dim counties
    we take the long calm
Lilting no haziness,
    sequel or psalm.

The little street wenches,
    the holy and clean,
Live as good neighbours live
    under the green.

Malice of sunbeam or
    menace of moon
Piping shall leave us
    no taste of a tune.

In the dim counties
    the eyelids are dumb,
To the lean citizens
    Love cannot come.

Love in the yellowing,
    Love at the turn,
Love o' the cooing lip –
    how should he burn?

The little street wenches,
    the callous, unclean
– Could they but tell us what
    all the gods mean.

Love cannot sabre us,
   blood cannot flow,
In the dim counties
   that wait us below.

## You, and Yellow Air

I dream of an old kissing-time
   And the flowered follies there;
In the dim place of cherry-trees,
   Of you, and yellow air.

It was an age of babbling,
   When the players would play
Mad with the wine and miracles
   Of a charmed holiday.

Bewildered was the warm earth
   With whistling and sighs,
And a young foal spoke all his heart
   With diamonds for eyes.

You were of Love's own colour
   In eyes and heart and hair;
In the dim place of cherry-trees
   Ridden by yellow air.

It was the time when red lovers
   With the red fevers burn;
A time of bells and silver seeds
   And cherries on the turn.

Children looked into tall trees
   And old eyes looked behind;
God in His glad October
   No sullen man could find.

Out of your eyes a magic
   Fell lazily as dew,
And every lad with lad's eyes
   Made summer love to you.

It was a reign of roses,
    Of blue flowers for the eye,
And the rustling of green girls
    Under a white sky.

I dream of an old kissing-time
    And the flowered follies there,
In the dim place of cherry-trees,
    Of you, and yellow air.


## Sheedy Was Dying

Grey as a rising ghost,
    Helpless and dumb;
This he had feared the most –
    Now it had come:
Through the tent door,
    Mocking, defying,
The Thirsty Land lay,
    – And Sheedy was dying!

Why should he ever
    Keep turning, keep turning
All his thoughts over
    To quicken their burning?
Why should the North wind speak.
    Creeping and crying?
– Who else could mourn for him?
    Sheedy was dying!

Ay! he had travelled far –
    Homeless, a rover;
Drunk his good share and more
    Half the world over;
So now had ended
    All toiling and trying:
Out in his tent alone
    Sheedy was dying!

Never a priest to make
　　Prayer to his travel
Out to that mist of things
　　None may unravel.
Steering out, staring out,
　　And the wind crying,
Who else could mourn for him,
　　Sheedy was dying.

Kind, in a surly way;
　　Somewhat rough-spoken;
Truth to his fellow-men
　　Keeping unbroken;
A strong man, he stood without
　　Flinching or sighing –
Now, on his bunk alone,
　　Sheedy was dying!

Birds of the Thirsty Land
　　In the dull grey…
Mist of the even-time
　　Floating away…
Still did the North wind speak,
　　Creeping and crying:
White, with his mouth agape,
　　Sheedy was dying!

## *May*

Shyly the silver-hatted mushrooms make
　　Soft entrance through,
And undelivered lovers, half awake,
　　Hear noises in the dew.

Yellow in all the earth and in the skies,
　　The world would seem
Faint as a widow mourning with soft eyes
　　And falling into dream.

Up the long hill I see the slow plough leave
    Furrows of brown;
Dim is the day and beautiful: I grieve
    To see the sun go down.

But there are suns a many for mine eyes
    Day after day:
Delightsome in grave greenery they rise,
    Red oranges in May.

## *Song Be Delicate*

Let your song be delicate.
    The skies declare
No war – the eyes of lovers
    Wake everywhere.

Let your voice be delicate.
    How faint a thing
Is Love, little Love crying
    Under the Spring.

Let your song be delicate.
    The flowers can hear:
Too well they know the tremble,
    Of the hollow year.

Let your voice be delicate.
    The bees are home:
All their day's love is sunken
    Safe in the comb.

Let your song be delicate.
    Sing no loud hymn:
Death is abroad... oh, the black season!
    The deep – the dim!

# The Prince Has Been into the Lane

How soft are the neighbours, they no more complain
At the noise of the children, the Prince has been into the lane.

How faint was the little one, how tired out and thin;
And the Prince was so proud and so distant; 'twas good of the Prince to
come in.

He who can stay the hot foot, and the heat in the brain,
He did delay for a moment; the Prince has been into the lane.

No monarch has ever been powerful to stay His decree,
They tell that He lives on black rivers across a wide sea.

Pity He has not; and yet He has put out a pain,
He stayed not a moment; the Prince has been into the lane.

'Twas kind of the Prince of the Shadows; He had far to come;
The awe of this honour – it leaves us half-hidden and dumb.

The little one knew but the footway, the dust, and the rain,
The hard word; the kind word – the Prince has been into the lane.

He has not the leisure for pity by night or by day –
Oh, thank the good Prince, as He hastened He made the delay.

Can He be older than Love? we see not an end to His reign,
Is he kinsman of God? or a vassal? – The Prince has been into the lane.

# The Sundowner

I know not when this tiresome man
With his shrewd, sable billy-can
    And his unwashed Democracy
His boomed-up Pilgrimage began.

Sometimes he wandered far outback
On a precarious Tucker Track;
    Sometimes he lacked Necessities
No gentleman would like to lack.

Tall was the grass, I understand,
When the old Squatter ruled the land.
    Why were the Conquerors kind to him?
Ah, the Wax Matches in his hand!

Where bullockies with oaths intense
Made of the dragged-up trees a fence,
    Gambling with scorpions he rolled
His Swag, conspicuous, immense.

In the full splendour of his power
Rarely he touched one mile an hour,
    Dawdling at sundown, History says,
For the Pint Pannikin of flour.

Seldom he worked; he was, I fear,
Unreasonably slow and dear;
    Little he earned, and that he spent
Deliberately drinking Beer.

Cheerful, sorefooted child of chance,
Swiftly we knew him at a glance;
    Boastful and self-compassionate,
Australia's Interstate Romance.

Shall he not live in Robust Rhyme,
Soliloquies and Odes Sublime?
    Strictly between ourselves, he was
A rare old Humbug all the time.

In many a Book of Bushland dim
Mopokes shall give him greeting grim;
    The old swans pottering in the reeds
Shall pass the time of day to him.

On many a page our Friend shall take
Small sticks his evening fire to make;
    Shedding his waistcoat, he shall mix
On its smooth back his Johnny-Cake.

'Mid the dry leaves and silvery bark
Often at nightfall will he park
    Close to a homeless creek, and hear
The Bunyip paddling in the dark.

## The Happy Thief

Who steals a kiss, he shall not ever rue it,
But he who buys, he bargains with the Devil.
Who steals a kiss shall move in merry places;
In all his days he shall see angel faces,
Nor ever shall he sink to earth's low level.
The Spring his life shall take and quite renew it;
He shall go down to death with all the graces.


## From a Coffin

Wrapt in the yellow earth
    What should I fear?
Sour hate and shallow mirth
    Never come near.
Shape me no epitaph!
    Sugar no rhyme!
I had the heart to laugh
    Once on a time.


## In the Long Gown

I have not the long gowns,
They that increase
All forms of sorrows
As the willow trees.

Hilda takes not friend with her
From the little town;
'Tis the black journey
In the long gown.

She liked not the long gowns;
Nay, she did please
All eyes with little skirts
Lapping her knees.

On all pretty journeys
She made joy arise,
Joy in her toe-taps,
Truth in her eyes.

Today she knows not
Frolic or frown;
'Tis a great journey
In the long gown.


## To a Blonde Typist

*To a Young Girl in the Employ of Big Business*

Gently with dolls not long since you were playing,
But you must come the old hard laws obeying:
Come where the old Ass Business leads the braying.

Business is like Apollyon, somewhat sooty;
Child, you are heavenly, and it is my duty
Here to give salutation to a Beauty.

Britain, your speech is all too mild in cursing.
Who is this Thief we keep on reimbursing?
Who is this Tyrant we persist in nursing?

Business I see a serpent, cool, suspicious,
Slithering in slime and always most malicious,
Foe to the Arts and patron of the vicious.

Now for a change compare him to a Tumour
Full of all meanness, blackness, evil rumour,
Quickly effacing all good faith and humour.

Business, they tell us, is a stern probation
Good for the soul. Nay, child, it is starvation,
Always resulting in complete damnation.


**joy arise**: the manuscript is damaged; these two words are conjectural.

Nature is kind, but Business will outwit her
(Sweetheart, I am though sometimes somewhat bitter
Merely a tomtit with an extra twitter).

You, you have eyes to make the whole world sunny;
Deep in your soul there is mistrust of Money:
Sweet one, forgive me if I call you Honey.

Often your eyes will through the windows wander;
You should be out upon the hillside yonder;
Here in the haste we dare not let you ponder.

You should be out where all Good has beginnings,
Out where the rainbow sometimes has an innings,
Always in sunlight counting up your winnings.

Here in the old calamities of Clatter,
Here we assist in making flatness flatter;
Here we insist that only dull things matter.

In a sane world who, who would rise at seven?
It should be ten, ten-thirty or eleven;
Life could be sung – a parody of Heaven.

Work should begin with wine and generous joking,
And in the place of penalties for smoking
Let us have fines for platitudes and croaking.

Honey, forgive me have I been offending;
All my old acts I should be now amending,
Chiefly with hymns to ease my latter ending.

Business a Dragon is, still bent on harming
Virtue and Youth. He has become alarming...
Ah, you are saved, and by your own Prince Charming.

## You Cannot Go Down to the Spring

The song will deceive you, the scent will incite you to sing;
You clutch but you cannot discover: you cannot go down to the Spring.

The day will be painted with summer, the heat and the gold
Will give you no key to the blossom: the music is old.

It is at the edge of a promise, a far-away thing;
The green is the nest of all riddles: you cannot go down to the Spring.

The truth is too close to the sorrow; the song you would sing,
It cannot go into the fever: you cannot go down to the Spring.

## Lament for Laddie

They stole him craftily
With flowers and satin white;
They took my lad from me:
I struggling in the night
Found no fond words to say.
They bore him down the way
In flowers and satin white.

Long was my heart afraid –
He was so white and slim.
I cried not; God had made
The world about me dim;
I may not taste or touch
The lad who took so much
Of morning down with him.

# Take Down the Fiddle, Karl!

Men openly call you the enemy, call you the swine,
But all that they say to me never can make you a foeman of mine.
The rain has come over the mountains, the gullies have faded away;
Take down the fiddle, Karl! the little old impudent fiddle: the work is all
          done for the day.

The ganger sits down in the bar-room with money to spend,
And many will laugh at his loudness, and many will hail him as friend.
How strong the mist settles! it sinks in the souls of us all.
Take down the fiddle, Karl! the little old impudent fiddle that hangs on
          the peg on the wall.

We are tired of the jack-hammers' clatter, the rattle of stone,
The many who boast of their travels, the many who moan;
We are tired of the spoil and the spoilers, the lifting of clay:
Take down the fiddle, Karl! the little old impudent fiddle: the work is all
          over today.

Your fiddle will show me your fathers, the hunt of the boar;
How dark were the forests! but fairies were seen at the door;
And in the old chapel your fathers bareheaded they came in to pray:
Take down the fiddle, Karl! the little old impudent fiddle: the work is all
          over today.

The fiddle is old but the things it is saying will ever be young;
It goes out and tries to be saying what cannot be sung.
The speech that you have, Karl, to me it means nothing at all:
Take down the fiddle, Karl! the little old impudent fiddle that hangs on
          the peg on the wall.

The fiddle can give us no more than the drinking of wine;
It brings up a world of good fellows to your eyes and mine.
The ganger, poor man, is misguided, his world is so grey:
Take down the fiddle, Karl! the little old impudent fiddle: the work is all
          done for the day.

# The Power of the Bells

The great bells grow not weary,
They call unto prayer;
They defeat well the Dark One
In the holy air.

With the reposing raiment
Of the fallen sun,
Softly they still discourage
That Evil One:

The Bat, the deep-fallen
Who craves mankind,
Who puts out his evil on
The opening mind.

The sweet bells persuade us
In the scent of the green
To keep back the Black One
Who rides unseen.

More than all violins
They entreat the sky,
The cool trees, the tall temples,
The pilgrims near by.

They compel the bleak Winter
To embrace the Spring;
In all joy they banish
That Evil Thing.

As moths move, the mystics
Above the hay,
So give they of gladness
On the bride's day.

As children, the innocent
In the whistling Spring,
In beauty they banish
The deformed Thing.

JOHN SHAW NEILSON

To the lanes of sorrow
They translate the sun;
They toll the defeat of
The Evil One.


## *To the Red Lory*

At the full face of the forest lies our little town:
Do thou from thy lookout to heaven, O lory, come down!

Come, charge with thy challenge of colour our thoughts cool and thin;
Descend with the blood of the sunlight – O lory, come in!

The clouds are away, 'tis October, the glees have begun;
Thy breast has the valour of music, O passionate one!

The rhythm is shine, the beloved, the unreason of Spring.
How royal thy raiment! No sorrow is under thy wing.

O thou of intrepid apparel, thy song is thy gown;
Translate thy proud speech of the sunlight – O lory, come down!


## *Uncle to a Pirate*

Often at eventide we go
To a tempestuous picture-show.
Gently I hold his heedless hand
In that preposterous Wonderland.

Pistols we see and big blue knives,
Bad men in trouble with their wives;
Burglars intruding; Life and Death,
And Humbug struggling for his breath.

Still he has hair of baby gold,
A Pirate nearly eight years old.
Oh, but his eyes! I am, I fear,
An uncle to a Buccaneer.

When the Pure Woman in the play
Is in distress he shouts 'Hooray!'
But when the keyed-up Villain dies
Tears have uprisen in his eyes.

Sometimes I feebly go with him
To the Old Centuries grave and dim;
Almost at times I understand
His muttering to a blood-red band.

Deep he goes down through mysteries,
Fearless he rides the ungoverned seas;
He with a gesture of his sword
Waves the uncounted gold aboard.

Any who would his will defy
Meet with no pity – all must die.
Proudly he hears them as they drown
Gurgling and cursing – all go down.

\* \* \*

Ah, it is gone! – the street again,
Hustling of women, noise of men,
The young girls simmering for a joke,
The keen lads in the lighted smoke.

How hopeful is the street! We stop
At his beloved folly-shop:
Oh, but his eyes! I am, I fear,
An uncle to a Buccaneer.

# The Bard and the Lizard

The lizard leans in to October,
    He walks on the yellow and green,
The world is awake and unsober,
    It knows where the lovers have been:
The wind, like a violoncello,
    Comes up and commands him to sing:
He says to me, 'Courage, good fellow!
    We live by the folly of Spring!'

A fish that the sea cannot swallow,
    A bird that can never yet rise,
A dreamer no dreamer can follow,
    The snake is at home in his eyes.
He tells me the paramount treason,
    His words have the resolute ring:
'Away with the homage to Reason!
    We live by the folly of Spring!'

The leaves are about him; the berry
    Is close in the red and the green,
His eyes are too old to be merry,
    He knows where the lovers have been.
And yet he could never be bitter,
    He tells me no sorrowful thing:
'The Autumn is less than a twitter!
    We live by the folly of Spring!'

As green as the light on a salad
    He leans in the shade of a tree,
He has good breath of a ballad,
    The strength that is down in the sea.
How silent he creeps in the yellow –
    How silent! and yet can he sing:
He gives me, 'Good morning, good fellow!
    We live by the folly of Spring!'

I scent the alarm of the faded
   Who love not the light and the play,
I hear the assault of the jaded,
   I hear the intolerant bray.
My friend has the face of a wizard,
   He tells me no desolate thing:
I learn from the heart of the lizard,
   We live by the folly of Spring!


## Dolly's Offering

Dolly has fashioned a wee bird home – two white eggs in a nest:
I dare not laugh at a holy thing, or a place where the young may rest:
Rude it is, but the mother love in Dolly beats home to me:
It shouts aloud of the heights of love and the wells of its melody.

Lips and eyes in the summer time and the faintest feet are bold:
Colours come to the heart and sing the song that is young and old:
The skies salute and the winds salute and the face of the earth is kind –
But Dolly can never come out to see, for Dolly is lame and blind.

Dolly is wise at eleven years old, for the dark has been her law:
Her body is put in a frozen place that only a love can thaw:
Love is keen in this that her two little hands have wrought for me:
It tells of wooing and joy and pain, and the pulse of the greenery.

I go out where the joys awake and the glistening lovers talk;
Joy is there in the young bird's flight and joy in the young child's talk;
Joys alight with the honey bees at the gates of the honey comb;
But 'tis a piece of the endless dark where Dolly is chained at home.

Dolly is all for love, it speaks in a thousand ways and shrill:
A home she heats with a good red heart, as a woman ever will:
The poor little nest is lined with love as warm as a man may find:
Out of the blackness light is called – and Dolly is lame and blind.

# The Eleventh Moon

'Twas in the eleventh moon I went
    wool gathering in the dim,
Near by me was a lover lad
    and the sweetness was on him.

Lightly his eyes went to the east
    and he with joy was dumb,
His sweet love walked a miracle
    out of the moonlight come.

Oh, but he was the fine lover!
    with a lover's thirsting eye:
– When two hearts beat the tune is sweet
    and knows not how to die.

Her laugh it was the rainbow's laugh
    delicious to the land,
And she gave to him for close loving
    her little silken hand.

Her face was made of Summer thought
    joined with the giddy Spring:
Gently I said, O heart, she is
    too heavenly a thing.

The moon did seem as music spilled
    upon her spotless gown,
And at her height of happiness
    the summer tear came down.

Night – and the silence honey-wet:
    the moon came to the full:
It was a time for gentle thought
    and the gathering of wool.

## Surely God Was a Lover

Surely God was a lover when He bade the day begin
Soft as a woman's eyelid – white as a woman's skin.

Surely God was a lover, with a lover's faults and fears,
When He made the sea as bitter as a wilful woman's tears.

Surely God was a lover, with the madness love will bring:
He wrought while His love was singing, and put her soul in the Spring.

Surely God was a lover, by a woman's wile controlled,
When He made the Summer a woman thirsty and unconsoled.

Surely God was a lover when He made the trees so fair;
In every leaf is a glory caught from a woman's hair.

Surely God was a lover – see, in the flowers He grows,
His love's eyes in the violet – her sweetness in the rose.


## The Poor Can Feed the Birds

Ragged, unheeded, stooping, meanly shod,
The poor pass to the pond; not far away
The spires go up to God.

Shyly they come from the unpainted lane;
Coats have they made of old unhappiness
That keeps in every pain.

The rich have fear, perchance their God is dim;
'Tis with the hope of stored-up happiness
They build the spires to Him.

The rich go out in clattering pomp and dare
In the most holy places to insult
The deep Benevolence there.

But 'tis the poor who make the loving words.
Slowly they stoop; it is a sacrament:
The poor can feed the birds.

Old, it is old, this scattering of the bread,
Deep as forgiveness, or the tears that go
Out somewhere to the dead.

The feast of love, the love that is the cure
For all indignities – it reigns, it calls,
It chains us to the pure.

Seldom they speak of God, He is too dim;
So without thought of after happiness
They feed the birds for Him.

The rich men walk not here on the green sod,
But they have builded towers, the timorous
That still go up to God.

Still will the poor go out with loving words;
In the long need, the need for happiness
The poor can feed the birds.


## *The Smoker Parrot*

He has the full moon on his breast,
The moonbeams are about his wing;
He has the colours of a king.
I see him floating unto rest
When all eyes wearily go west,
And the warm winds are quieting.
The moonbeams are about his wing:
He has the full moon on his breast.

# *Lesbia Harford*
## 1891–1927

Lesbia Harford, born Keogh, suffered from a congenital heart defect which sapped her energy, but through sheer will-power she managed to live a full if short life on her own terms. Her father deserted the family early, and was only rarely heard from after that; this made life a struggle for them and it was a triumph on their part that Lesbia could attend Catholic boarding schools and the University of Melbourne. She graduated from the latter with one of the first law degrees it ever conferred on a woman. As a member of the radical organisation Industrial Workers of the World, she chose not to follow a legal career, but worked in clothing and textile factories. At times a fellow activist had to cover for her lack of productivity, caused by ill health. In 1918 she moved to Sydney to live with the family of an imprisoned IWW member and help support them. She worked as a factory machinist and then as a domestic servant for the Fairfax family of newspaper proprietors. In 1920 she married an artist named Harford, who took more and more to alcohol as his career failed. This, and violence, brought the marriage to an end after a few years, though she always defended him from those who condemned him. When the IWW collapsed, she did not follow the move of many of its members into the ranks of the Communist party; one of them remarked kindly enough that she was not a natural Communist. She wrote a novel, *The Invaluable Mystery*, about the treatment of Germans and radicals in Australia during the First World War; this was lost for sixty years, and only discovered and published in 1987. By 1925 she was back in Melbourne and had taken a job as an articled clerk. Her health then failed increasingly, and a bacterial infection of the heart killed her in 1927.

Lesbia Harford's poems make no effort to hide her bisexuality, and she was opposed on ideological grounds to what she thought of as elitist art. As an example, she rejected classical music and valued only brass bands. In poetry, her political ideals allowed her consistently to avoid the dead Victorianisms which afflicted Australian poetry well into the twentieth century. Some of her poetry appeared in radical magazines, and a special issue of a literary magazine was devoted to her work during her lifetime. After her death a small volume of her poems appeared, and then she was very largely forgotten until the 1980s. In 1985 a definitive scholarly edition of her work appeared, edited by Drusilla Modjeska and Marjorie Pizer, and I am indebted to that book for the dating of Harford's poems, which made a chronological selection possible.

## [I dreamt last night]

I dreamt last night
That spring had come.
Across green fields I saw a blur
Of crimson-blossomed plum.

I've never known
So fair a thing.
And yet I wish it were a dream
Of some forgotten spring.

Today the sun
Our workroom blest
And there was hard young wattle pinned
On our forewoman's breast.

## [If I had six white horses]

If I had six white horses
And six sturdy friends,
I'd sell them into slavery,
If that would gain your ends.

I'd sell them into slavery,
If you so willed.
Thus were the hearts blood o' the world
By treason spilled.

## Little Ships

The little ships are dearer than the great ships
For they sail in strange places,
They lean nearer the green waters.
One may count by wavelets how the year slips
From their decks; and hear the Sea-King's daughters
Laughing at their play whene'er the boat dips.

## [I count the days until I see you, dear]

I count the days until I see you, dear,
But the days only.
I dare not reckon up the nights and hours
I shall be lonely.

But when at last I meet you, dearest heart,
How can it cheer me?
Desire has power to turn me into stone,
When you come near me.

I give my heart the lie against my will,
Seem not to see you,
Glance aside quickly if I meet your eye,
Love you and flee you.


## [I can't feel the sunshine]

I can't feel the sunshine
Or see the stars aright
For thinking of her beauty
And her kisses bright.

She would let me kiss her
Once and not again.
Deeming soul essential,
Sense doth she disdain.

If I should once kiss her,
I would never rest
Till I had lain hour long
Pillowed on her breast.

Lying so, I'd tell her
Many a secret thing
God has whispered to me
When my soul took wing.

Would that I were Sappho,
Greece my land, not this!
There the noblest women,
When they loved, would kiss.

## [My mission in the world]

My mission in the world
Is to prolong
Rapture by turning it
Into a song.

A song of liberty
Bound by no rule!
No marble meaning's mine
Fixed for a school.

My singing ecstasy
Winged for the flight,
Each will hear differently,
And hear aright.

## Day's End

Little girls,
    You are gay,
Little factory girls,
At the end of your day.

There you stand,
    Huddled close,
On the back of a tram,
Having taken your dose.

And you go
    Through the grey
And the gold of the streets
At the close of the day,

Blind as moles.
    You are crude,
You are sweet, little girls,
And amazingly rude,

But so fine
    To be gay.
Gentle people are dull
At the end of the day.

## [Ours was a friendship in secret, my dear]

Ours was a friendship in secret, my dear,
    Stolen from fate.
I must be secret still, show myself calm
    Early and late.

'Isn't it sad he was killed!' I must hear
    With a smooth face.
'Yes, it is sad.' – Oh, my darling, my own
    My heart of grace.

## [Somebody brought in lilac]

Somebody brought in lilac,
Lilac after rain.
Isn't it strange, belovéd of mine
You'll not see it again?

Lilac glad with the sun on it
Flagrant fair from birth,
Mourns in colour, belovéd of mine,
You laid in the earth.

## Deliverance Through Art

When I am making poetry I'm good
And happy then.
I live in a deep world of angelhood
Afar from men.
And all the great and bright and fiery troop
Kiss me agen
With love.    Deathless Ideas!    I have no need
Of girls' lips then.

Goodness and happiness and poetry,
I put them by.
I will not rush with great wings gloriously
Against the sky
While poor men sit in holes, unbeautiful,
Unsouled, and die:
Better let misery and pettiness
Make me their sty.

## The Folk I Love

I do hate the folk I love,
They hurt so.
Their least word and act may be
Source of woe.

Won't you come to tea with me?'
'Not today.
I'm so tired, I've been to church.'
Such folk say.

All the dreary afternoon
I must clutch
At the strength to love like them,
Not too much.

## [Oh, oh Rosalie]

Oh, oh Rosalie,
Oh, oh Rosalie,
What would you have of me?
Oh, oh Rosalie.

I have kisses fine,
I have kisses fine.
Will you take kiss of mine?
Oh, oh Rosalie.

I have dreams in store,
I have dreams in store,
Fine spun as lace of yore.
Oh, oh Rosalie.

Many a mighty thought,
Many a mighty thought
By men of old time wrought
Is mine, Rosalie.

I have golden days,
I have golden days,
Green trees, and leafy ways.
Oh, oh Rosalie.

I have tears for you,
I have tears for you,
And roses filled with dew.
Oh, oh Rosalie.

Oh, oh Rosalie,
What do you want of me?
You would have nought of me.
Oh, oh Rosalie.


## *[All day long]*

All day long
We sew fine muslin up for you to wear,
Muslin that women wove for you elsewhere,
A million strong.

Just like flames,
Insatiable, you eat up all our hours
And sun and loves and tea and talk and flowers
Suburban dames.

# Fatherless

I've had no man
To guard and shelter me,
Guide and instruct me
From mine infancy.

No lord of earth
To show me day by day
What things a girl should do
And what she should say.

I have gone free
Of manly excellence
And hold their wisdom
More than half pretence.

For since no male
Has ruled me or has fed,
I think my own thoughts
In my woman's head.


# Lawstudent and Coach

Each day I sit in an ill-lighted room
To teach a boy;
For one hour by the clock great words and dreams
Are our employ.

We read *St Agnes' Eve* and that more fair
*Eve of St Mark*
At a small table up against the wall
In the half-dark.

I tell him all the wise things I have read
Concerning Keats.
'His earlier work is overfull of sense
And sensual sweets.'

I tell him all that comes into my mind
From God-knows-where,
 Remark, 'In English poets Bertha's type
Is jolly rare.

She's a real girl that strains her eyes to read
And cricks her neck.
Now Madeline could pray all night nor feel
Her body's check.

And Bertha *reads,* p'rhaps the first reading girl
In English rhyme.'
It's maddening work to say what Keats has said
A second time.

The boy sits sideways with averted head.
His brown cheek glows.
I like his black eyes and his sprawling limbs
And his short nose.

He, feeling, dreads the splendour of the verse,
But he must learn
To write about it neatly and to quote
These lines that burn.

He drapes his soul in my obscuring words
Makes himself fit
To go into a sunny world and take
His part in it.

'Examiners' point of view, you know,' say I,
'Is commonsense.
You must sift poetry before you can
Sift Evidence.'

# Machinists Talking

I sit at my machine
Hourlong beside me, Vera, aged nineteen,
Babbles her sweet and innocent tale of sex.

Her boy, she hopes, will prove
Unlike his father in the act of love.
Twelve children are too many for her taste.

She looks sidelong, blue-eyed,
And tells a girlish story of a bride
With the sweet licence of Arabian queens.

Her child, she says, saw light
Minute for minute, nine months from the night
The mother first lay in her lover's arms.

She says a friend of hers
Is a man's mistress who gives jewels and furs
But will not have her soft limbs cased in stays.

I open my small store
And tell of a young delicate girl, a whore,
Stole from her mother many months ago.

Fate made the woman seem
To have a tiger's loveliness, to gleam
Strong and fantastic as a beast of prey.

I sit at my machine.
Hourlong beside me, Vera, aged nineteen,
Babbles her sweet and innocent tale of sex.

# The Invisible People

When I go into town at half past seven
Great crowds of people stream across the ways,
Hurrying, although it's only half past seven.
They are the invisible people of the days.

When you go in to town about eleven
The hurrying, morning crowds are hid from view.
Shut in the silent buildings at eleven
They toil to make life meaningless for you.

# Closing Time: Public Library

At ten o'clock the great gong sounds its dread
Prelude to splendour. I push back my chair,
And all the people leave their books. We flock,
Still acquiescent, down the marble stair
Into the dark where we can't read. And thought
Swoops down insatiate through the starry air.

# Machinist's Song

The foot of my machine
Sails up and down
Upon the blue of this fine lady's gown.

Sail quickly, little boat,
With gifts for me,
Night and the goldy streets and liberty.

# Periodicity

My friend declares
Being woman and virgin she
Takes small account of periodicity

And she is right.
Her days are calmly spent
For her sex-function is irrelevant.

But I whose life
Is monthly broke in twain
Must seek some sort of meaning in my pain.

Women, I say,
Are beautiful in change,
Remote, immortal, like the moon they range.

Or call my pain
A skirmish in the whole
Tremendous conflict between body and soul.

Meaning must lie,
Some beauty surely dwell
In the fierce depths and uttermost pits of hell.

Yet still I seek,
Month after month in vain,
Meaning and beauty in recurrent pain.


## [This evening I'm alone]

This evening I'm alone.
I wish there'd be
Someone to come along
And talk to me.

Yet out of all my friends
There isn't one
I'd like to come and talk
To me alone.

But if a stranger came
With newer brain
We'd yarn until we felt
Alive again.


## *[I was sad]*

I was sad
Having signed up in a rebel band,
Having signed up to rid the land
Of a plague it had.

For I knew
That I would suffer, I would be lost,
Be bitter and foolish and tempest tost
And a failure too.

I was sad;
Though far in the future our light would shine
For the present the dark was ours, was mine,
I couldn't be glad.


## *[All through the day at my machine]*

All through the day at my machine
There still keeps going
A strange little tune through heart and head
As I sit sewing:
    'There is a child in Hungary,
    A child I love in Hungary'
The words come flowing.

When I am walking home at night
That song comes after,
And under the trees in holiday time
Or hearing laughter:
    'I have a son in Hungary,
    My little son in Hungary'
Comes following after.

## [Sometimes I wish that I were Helen-fair]

Sometimes I wish that I were Helen-fair
And wise as Pallas,
That I might have most royal gifts to pour
In love's sweet chalice.

Then I reflect my dear love is no god
But mortal only
And in this heavenly wife might deem himself
Not blest, but lonely.


## [Sometimes I am too tired]

Sometimes I am too tired
To think of you.
Today was such a day,
But then I knew
Today, for certain, you'd be weary too.

You there in hospital
With health to seek –
And me at my machine
Too tired to speak –
We're very funny lovers of a week.


## [My lovely pixie, my good companion]

My lovely pixie, my good companion,
You do not love me, bed-mate of mine,
Save as a child loves,
Careless of loving,
Rather preferring raspberry wine.

How can you help it? You were abandoned.
Your mother left you. Your father died.
All your young years of
Pain and desertion
Are not forgotten, here at my side.

# [Into old rhyme]

Into old rhyme
The new words come but shyly.
Here's a brave man
Who sings of commerce dryly.

Swift-gliding cars
Through town and country winging,
Like cigarettes,
Are deemed unfit for singing.

Into old rhyme
New words come tripping slowly.
Hail to the time
When they possess it wholly.

# [The love I look for]

The love I look for
Could not come from you.
My mind is set to fall
At Peterloo.
But you'ld protect me,
I'd be safe with you.

You could but love me
In the olden way,
With gifts of jewels, children,
Time to play,
Be man to woman
In the olden way.

The love that's love has
Other gifts to bring,
A share in weakness, dreams,
And suffering.
These are the only
Gifts I'd have to bring.

The love I look for
Does not come from you.
I see it dawning in
Deep eyes of blue.
I dare to hope for
Love, but not from you.


## [He has a fairy wife]

He has a fairy wife.
He does not know her.
She is the heart of the storm,
Of the clouds that lower.

And as the clouds are torn
Into rain and thunder,
She in her brightness tears
His heart asunder.


## [Those must be masts of ships the gazer sees]

Those must be masts of ships the gazer sees
On through the little gap in the park trees
So far away that seeing almost fails.
Those must be masts, the lovely masts of ships
Stripped bare of sails.

There's nothing here to please the seeing eyes,
Four poles with crossway beams against the skies.
But beauty's not for sight. True beauty sings
Of latent movement to the unsensed soul
In love with wings.

## [I have golden shoes]

I have golden shoes
To make me fleet.
They are like the wind
Underneath my feet.

When my lover's kiss
Is overbold,
I can run away
In my shoes of gold.

Nay, when I am shod
With this bright fire,
I am forced to run
From my own desire.

From the love I love
Whose arms enfold
I must run away
In my shoes of gold.

## [Now I've been three days]

Now I've been three days
In the place where I am staying,
I've taken up new ways –
Land-owning and flute playing.

There's an orchard ground
Seen, that set me sighing.
Should I give ten pounds,
It is mine for the buying.

With the door set wide,
I could sit there playing,
Send the magic notes
Through the gully straying.

Since the roof is sound
And the trees are growing,
I will give ten pounds,
All my gold bestowing.

Now I've been three days
In the place where I am staying,
I've taken up new ways –
Land-owning and flute playing.


## [I found an orchid in the valley fair]

I found an orchid in the valley fair,
And named it for us both,
And left it there.

Two flowers upon one stem, white-souled, alone.
I couldn't pull them up,
And bring them home.


## [I love to see]

I love to see
Her looking up at me,
Stretched on a bed
In her pink dressing gown,
Her arms above her head,
Her hair all down.
I love to see
Her smiling up at me.

## Skirt Machinist

I am making great big skirts
For great big women –
Amazons who've fed and slept
Themselves inhuman.

Such long skirts, not less than two
And forty inches.
Thirty round the waist for fear
The webbing pinches.

There must be tremendous tucks
On those round bellies.
Underneath the limbs will shake
Like wine-soft jellies.

I am making such big skirts
And all so heavy,
I can see their wearers at
A lord–mayor's levee.

I, who am so small and weak
I have hardly grown,
Wish the skirts I'm making less
Unlike my own.


## [I'm like all lovers]

I'm like all lovers, wanting love to be
A very mighty thing for you and me.

In certain moods your love should be a fire
That burnt your very life up in desire.

The only kind of love then to my mind
Would make you kiss my shadow on the blind

And walk seven miles each night to see it there.
Myself within, serene and unaware.

But you're as bad. You'd have me watch the clock
And count your coming while I mend your sock.

You'd have my mind devoted day and night
To you and care for you and your delight.

Poor fools, who each would have the other give
What spirit must withhold if it would live.

You're not my slave, I wish you not to be.
I love yourself and not your love for me,

The self that goes ten thousand miles away
And loses thought of me for many a day.

And you loved me for loving much beside
But now you want a woman for your bride.

Oh, make no woman of me, you who can,
Or I will make a husband of a man.

By my unwomanly love that sets you free
Love all myself, but least the woman in me.


## [I used to be afraid]

I used to be afraid to meet
The lovers going down our street.

I'd try to shrink to half my size
And blink and turn away my eyes

But now I'm one of them I know
I never need have bothered so.

And they won't mind it if I stare
Because they'll never know I'm there

Or if they do, they're proud to be
Fond lovers for the world to see.

## Body and Soul

Through the Museum
I stroll, and see
Goblets fashioned in Arcady,
Spears from the Islands, and robes from Tyre –
Gew-gaws of pomp and of old desire.

On one of the walls
A looking glass
Catches my image as I pass.
Austerely from mirrored eyes, I see
The soul of the past look out at me.

## A Blouse Machinist

Miss Murphy has blue eyes and blue-black hair,
Her machine's opposite mine
So I can stare
At her pale face and shining blue-black hair.

I'm sure that other people think her plain
But I could look at her
And look again
Although I see why people think her plain.

She's nice to watch when her machine-belt breaks.
She has such delicate hands
And arms, it takes
Ages for her to mend it when it breaks.

Oh, beauty's still elusive and she's fine.
Though all the moulding
Of her face, the line
Of nose, mouth, chin is Mongol, yet she's fine.

Of course things would be different in Japan.
They'd see her beauty.
On a silken fan
They'd paint her for a princess in Japan.

But still her loveliness eludes the blind.
They never use their eyes
But just their mind.
So must much loveliness elude the blind.

## An Improver

Maisie's been holding down her head all day,
Her little red head. And her pointed chin
Rests on her neck that slips so softly in
The square-cut low-necked darling dress she made
In such a way, since it's high-waisted too,
It lets you guess how fair young breasts begin
Under the gentle pleasant folds of blue.

But on the roof at lunchtime when the sun
Shone warmly and the wind was blowing free
She lifted up her head to let me see
A little rosy mark beneath the chin –
The mark of kisses. If her mother knew
She'd be ashamed, but a girl-friend like me
Made her feel proud to show her kisses to.

## [Once I thought my love]

Once I thought my love was worth the name
If tears came.

When the wound is mortal, now I know
Few tears flow.

## [Pink eucalyptus flowers]

Pink eucalyptus flowers
(The flowers are out)
Are scented honey sweet
For bees to buzz about.

Pink eucalyptus flowers
(The flowers are out)
Are fair as any rose
For us to sing about.

## [I came to live in Sophia Street]

I came to live in Sophia Street,
In a little house in Sophia Street
With an inch of floor
Between door and door
And a yard you'd measure in children's feet.
When I'd been ten days in Sophia Street
I remembered its name was Wisdom Street;
For I'd learned much more
Than in all the score
Of years I clamoured for books to eat.

## [Today is rebels' day]

Today is rebels' day. And yet we work –
All of us rebels, until day is done.
And when the stars come out we celebrate
A revolution that's not yet begun.

Today is rebels' day. And men in jail
Tread the old mill-round until day is done.
And when night falls they sit alone to brood
On revolution that's not yet begun.

Today is rebels' day. Let all of us
Take courage to fight on until we're done –
Fight though we may not live to see the hour
The Revolution's splendidly begun.

## [To look across at Moira]

To look across at Moira gives me pleasure.
She has a red tape measure.

Her dress is black and all the workroom's dreary,
And I am weary.

But that's like blood – like a thin blood stream trickling –
Like a fire quickening.

It's Revolution. Ohé, I take pleasure
In Moira's red tape measure.


## Street Music

There's a band in the street, there's a band in the street.
It will play you a tune for a penny –
It will play you a tune, you a tune, you a tune,
And you, though you haven't got any,

For the music's free, and the music's bold.
It cannot really be bought and sold.

And the people walk with their heads held high
Whether or not they've a penny.
And the music's there as the bandsmen know,
For the poor though the poor are many.

Oh the music's free and the music's bold.
It cannot really be bought and sold.

## [I dreamt last night of happy home-comings]

I dreamt last night of happy home-comings.
Friends I had loved and had believed were dead
Came happily to visit me and said
I was a part of their fair home-coming.

It's strange that I should dream of welcomings
And happy meetings when my love, last week
Returned from exile, did not even speak
Or write to me or need my welcoming.


## [The happiest of love's moments]

Sometimes I think the happiest of love's moments
Is the blest moment of release from loving.

The world once more is all one's own to model
Upon one's own and not another's pattern.

And each poor heart imprisoned by the other's
Is suddenly set free for splendid action.

For no two lovers are a single person
And lovers' union means a soul's suppression.

Oh, happy then the moment of love's passing
When those strong souls we sought to slay recover.


## [The people have drunk the wine of peace]

The people have drunk the wine of peace
In the streets of town.
They smile as they drift with hearts at rest
Uphill and down.

The people have drunk the wine of peace,
They are mad with joy.
Never again need they lie and fear
Death for a boy.

## Girl's Love

I lie in the dark
Grass beneath and you above me,
Curved like the sky,
Insistent that you love me.

But the high stars
Admonish to refuse you
And I'm for the stars
Though in the stars I lose you.

## [I must be dreaming through the days]

I must be dreaming through the days
And see the world with childish eyes
If I'd go singing all my life
And my songs be wise

And in the kitchen or the house
Must wonder at the sights I see.
And I must hear the throb and hum
That moves to song in factory.

So much in life remains unsung,
And so much more than love is sweet.
I'd like a song of kitchenmaids
With steady fingers and swift feet.

And I could sing about the rest
That breaks upon a woman's day
When dinner's over and she lies
Upon her bed to dream and pray

Until the children come from school
And all her evening work begins.
There's more in life than tragic love
And all the storied, splendid sins.

## [When I get up to light the fire]

When I get up to light the fire,
And dress with all the speed I may
By candle-light, I dread the hours
That go to make a single day.

But then I leave my room, and see
How brightly, clearly darkness shines,
When stars ten thousand miles away
Are caught in our verandah vines.

And I am almost glad that fires
Have to be lit, before the day
Comes up between the trees and drives
The strange familiar dark away.


## [Today, in class]

Today, in class,
I read aloud to forty little boys
The legend of King Croesus' boasted joys.

They were so young,
Restless, and eager, I believed they'd find
This moral story little to their mind.

But they were pleased
With the old legend, quick to comprehend
Sorrowful wisdom's triumph at the end:

They seemed to feel,
In hush of wonder, hurry of amaze,
The sure uncertainty of all men's days.

## [I bought a red hat]

I bought a red hat
To please my lover.
He will hardly see it
When he looks me over.

Though it's a fine hat.
Yet he never misses
Noticing my red mouth
When it's shaped for kisses.

## Miss Mary Fairfax

Every day Miss Mary goes her rounds,
Through the splendid house and through the grounds,

Looking if the kitchen table's white,
Seeing if the great big fire's alight,

Finding specks on shining pans and pots,
Never praising much, but scolding lots.

If the table's white, she does not see
Roughened hands that once were ivory.

It is fires, not cheeks, that ought to glow;
And if eyes are dim, she doesn't know.

Poor Miss Mary! Poor for all she owns,
Since the things she loves are stocks and stones.

## [Whenever I think of you]

Whenever I think of you, you are alone,
Shut by yourself between
Great walls of stone.

There is a stool, I think, and a table there,
And a mat underneath your feet;
And the rest is bare.

I cannot stop remembering this, my own,
Seventeen hours of the day
You are alone.

## A Strike Rhyme

The strike's done.
The men won.
The ships sail the sea
To bring back
What we lack,
Coal, sugar, tea.

And I'm glad,
Though I had
Rather never use
Tea and spice
And what's nice
Than see the men lose.

## [In this little school]

In this little school
Life goes so sweetly,
Day on azure day
Is lost completely.

No one thinks too much,
Or worries greatly.
In a pleasant shade
We dream sedately.

There's no struggle here
Or conflict showing;
Only the sweet pain
Of young limbs growing.

# Inventory

We've a room
That we call home,
With a bed in it,
And a table
And some chairs,
A to Z in it.
There's a mirror,
And a safe,
And a lamp in it.
Were there more,
Our mighty love
Might get cramp in it.


# A Parlourmaid

'I want a parlourmaid.'
        'Well, let me see
If you were God, what kind of maid she'd be.'

'She would be tall,
She would be fair,
She would have slender limbs,
A delicate air;
And yet for all her beauty
She would walk
Among my guests unseen
And through their talk
Her voice would be the sweet voice of a bird,
Not listened to, though heard.'

'And now I know the girl you have in mind
Tell me her duties, if you'd be so kind.'

'Why, yes!
She must know names of wines
And never taste them –
Must handle fragile cups
And never break them –

HELL AND AFTER

Must fill my rooms with flowers
And never wear them –
Must serve my daughter's secrets
And not share them.'

'Madam, you are no God, that's plain to see.
I'll just repeat what you have said to me.

You say your maid must look in Helen fashion
Golden and white
And yet her loveliness inspire no passion,
Give no delight.

Your intimate goods of home must owe their beauty
To this girl's care
But she'll not overstep her path of duty
Nor seek to share

Through loving or enjoying or possessing
The least of them.
            Why, she's not human, by your own confessing,
And you condemn

Your rational self in every word you're speaking!
Please understand
You'll find the hollow maiden you are seeking
In fairyland.'

## Street Scene – Little Lonsdale St

I wish you'd seen that dirty little boy,
Finger at nose,
Peeking and ginking at some girls in rows
Seated on the high window-sills to rest.

One of the girls had hair as bright as corn.
And one was red.
And over their soft forms a glow was shed
From lamps new-lighted in the laundry there.

That boy, beneath them, wheeled a hand–cart full
Of cast-off busts
From sewing rooms. They looked like shells of lusts.
And all the girls around the windows laughed.


## [I'd like to spend long hours at home]

I'd like to spend long hours at home
With a small child to bother me.
I'd take her out to see the shops
And fuss about my husband's tea.

Instead of this I spend my days
In noisy schoolrooms, harsh and bare.
Unloved am I, since people give
Too many children to my care.


## [I had a lover who betrayed me]

I had a lover who betrayed me.
First he implored and then gainsaid me.

Hopeless I dared no more importune.
I found new friends, a kinder fortune.

Silence, indifference did greet me.
Twice in long years he's chanced to meet me.

Yet when I see him I discover
I was inconstant, he the lover.

# [*A way of making friends*]

Most people have a way of making friends
That's very queer.
They don't choose whom they like, but anyone
In some way *near*.

The girl beside them on the factory bench,
The girl next door
Does. If they move then they forget the friend
They had before.

I choose the friends who suit me (one I found
Shut up in jail) –
Some nuns, some clerks, Anne whose beauty was
Frankly for sale.

Of course I cannot see them every day
That's as Fate sends,
Blind Fate may choose my times for me, but not,
Oh not, my friends.


# The Psychological Craze

I in the library,
Looking for books to read,
Pulled one out twice to see
If it fulfilled my need.

Butler had written this
Autobiography.
Which of the Butlers, then?
I opened it to see.

He's an old general
Mounted upon a horse.
Thinkers don't write their lives,
But soldiers can, of course.

They write: 'The regiment
Was sent to Omdurman,
Where Gordon died. To catch
The Mahdi was our plan.'

Later – 'The bride wore white
And she had golden hair.
Four bridesmaids bore her train
Up to the altar where

His Grace of Birmingham' –
It's the old rigmarole,
Names, facts and dates – no word
In this about the soul.

No dreams, no sin, no tears!
Only the body thrives.
Upon such worthless things
Great soldiers base their lives.

No wonder wars are fought.
Loss of such life is small,
Life bound to space and time,
Not infinite at all.

## Lovers Parted

*'With the awakening of the memory of a forbidden action there is combined the
awakening of the tendency to carry out the action.'*

*Totem and Taboo*, S. Freud

Old memories waken old desires
Infallibly. While we're alive
With eye or ear or sense at all,
Sometimes, must love revive.

But we'll not think, when some stray gust
Relumes the flicker of desire,
That fuel of circumstance could make
A furnace of our fire.

The past is gone. We must believe
It has no power to change our lives.
Yet still our constant hearts rejoice
Because the past survives.


## 'All Knowledge...'

I know more about flowers,
And Pat knows about ships.
'Schooner' and 'barquentine'
Are words of note on his lips.

Even 'schooner, barque-rigged'
Has meaning for him. And yet
I don't believe he knows
Hearts' ease from mignonette.

And whenever the daffodils,
Like visiting golden dames,
Honour our humble flat,
He has to ask their names.


## [How funny it would be]

How funny it would be if dreamy I
Should leave one book behind me when I die
And that a book of Law – this silly thing
Just written for the money it will bring.
I do hope, when it's finished, I'll have time
For other books and better spurts of rhyme.

## [Pat wasn't Pat]

Pat wasn't Pat last night at all.
He was the rain,
The Spring,
Young Dionysus, white and warm,
Lilac and everything.

## [A bunch of lilac and a storm of hail]

A bunch of lilac and a storm of hail
On the same afternoon! Indeed I know
Here in the South it always happens so,
That lilac is companioned by the gale.

I took some hailstones from the window sill
And swallowed them in a communion feast.
Their transitory joy is mine at least,
The lilac's loveliness escapes me still.

Mine are the storms of spring, but not the sweets.

## [Oh you, dear trees]

O you, dear trees, you have learned so much of beauty,
You must have studied this only the ages long!
Men have thought of God and laughter and duty.
And of love. And of song.

But you, dear trees, from your birth to your hour of dying,
Have cared for this one way only of being wise.
Lovely, lovely, lovely, the sapling sighing.
Lovely the dead tree lies.

## [Last night, in a dream]

Last night, in a dream, I felt the peculiar anguish
Known to me of old;
And there passed me, not much changed, my earliest lover,
Smiling, suffering, cold.

This morning, I lay with closed lids under the blankets,
Lest with night depart
The truthful dream which restored to me with my lover
My passionate heart.


## White Sunshine

The sun's my fire.
Golden, from a magnificence of blue,
Should be its hue.

But woolly clouds,
Like boarding-house old ladies, come and sit
In front of it.

White sunshine, then,
That has the frosty glimmer of white hair,
Freezes the air.

They must forget,
So self-absorbed are they, so very old,
That I'll be cold.


## Flowers and Light

Flowers have uncountable ways of pretending to be
Not solid, but moonlight or sunlight or starlight with scent.
Primroses strive for the colour of sunshine on lawns
Dew-besprent.

Freesias are flames wherein light more than heat is desired,
As candles on altars burn amethyst, golden and white.
Wall-flowers are sun streaked with shade. Periwinkles blue noon
At the height.


## Pruning Flowering Gums

One summer day, along the street,
Men pruned the gums
To make them neat.
The tender branches, white with flowers,
Lay in the sun
For hours and hours,
And every hour they grew more sweet,
More honey-like
Until the street
Smelt like a hive, withouten bees.
But still the gardeners
Lopped the trees.

Then came the children out of school,
Noisy and separate
As their rule
Of being is. The spangled trees
Gave them one heart:
Such power to please
Had all the flowering branches strown
Around for them
To make their own.
Then such a murmuring arose
As made the ears
Confirm the nose
And give the lie to eyes. For hours
Child bees hummed
In the honey flowers.

They gathered sprigs and armfuls. Some
Ran with their fragrant
Burdens home,
And still returned; and after them
Would drag great boughs.
Some stripped a stem
Of rosy flowers and played with these.
Never such love
Had earthly trees
As these young creatures gave. By night,
The treasured sprays
Of their delight
Were garnered every one. The street
Looked, as the council liked it, neat.

## Polytheist

One comes to love the little saints,
As years go by.
One learns to love the little saints.
'O hear me sigh,
St Anthony,
Find this for me,
I wish you'd try.'

There must be many garden gods,
A gardener sees.
There'd have to be an orchard god.
'Divinities,
Take honour due.
The long year through
Protect these trees.'

The Mother and the Holy Child
Are friends to me.
I pray, 'I am my mother's child.
I trust you'll see
That days are bright
And all goes right
With her and me.'

## 'Love is not love...'

When I was still a child
I thought my love would be
Noble, truthful, brave,
And very kind to me.

Then all the novels said
That if my lover prove
No such man as this
He had to forfeit love.

Now I know life holds
Harder tasks in store.
If my lover fail
I must love him more.

Should he prove unkind,
What am I, that he
Squander soul and strength
Smoothing life for me?

Weak or false or cruel
Love must still be strong.
All my life I'll learn
How to love as long.


## The Moonlit Room

I know a room that's dark in daytime hours;
No sunbeams light it,
Whether in months of gloom or months of flowers,
So people slight it.

Yet in the noon of each succeeding night
The moon shines in it,
Goldenly waking dreamers to delight
For a love's minute.

In a dream light, they sigh and burn and kiss
And fall to slumber
Deeply once more. Thus bliss is piled on bliss
In goodly number.

Praise first is giv'n to sunshine and to rooms
Sunbright, with reason.
Yet a wise man should choose a moonlit room
In his blood's season.


## A Meaning Learnt

I'm not his wife. I am his paramour:
His wayside love, picked up in journeying:
Rose of the hedgerows: fragrant, till he fling
Me down beside the ditch, a droopéd thing
Some country boy may stick into his hat.
A paramour has no more use than that.


## The Wife

He's out of work!
I tell myself a change should mean a chance,
And he must look for changes to advance,
And he, of all men, really needs a jerk.

But I hate change.
I like my kitchen with its pans and pots
That shine like new although we've used them lots.
I wouldn't like a kitchen that was strange.

And it's not true
All changes are for better. Some are worse.
A man had rather work, though work's a curse,
Than mope at home with not a thing to do.

No surer thing
Than that he'll get another job. But soon!
Or else I'll have to change. This afternoon
Would be the time, before I sell my ring.

## Raiment

I cannot be tricked out in lovely clothes
All times, all days.
My mind has moods of hating pearl and rose
And jewel-blaze.

Nor is the body worthily attired
Unless the soul
Has visibly to nobleness aspired
And self-control.

## [When I am articled]

When I am articled
The Law decrees
I shall devote my time
To stating fees

And learning about Actions
Suits and Courts.
Then Deeds and Briefs and Grants
Must fill my thoughts.

While if a naughty
Little verse should find
Its way into a corner
Of my mind

I must not tell the chap
For whom I work.
He pays the penalty
If I should shirk.

And take to writing books
And verse instead
Of 'hereinafter', 'duly',
'Viz', 'the said'.

# [When my lover]

When my lover put the sea between us
And went wandering in Italy
My poor silly heart miscalled his journey –
'Leaving me'.

Towns of Spain and Italy he stayed in,
Each and all of them to me unknown;
How could he find pleasure being a lover,
Being alone!

Truly I was not as fair as Venice
Noble as Siena, strange as Rome.
Certainly he loved Milan and Florence
More than home.

I believed his absence had estranged us
And across the heart-dividing sea
Sent him word that I no longer loved him.
Foolish me!

Came his answer after months of waiting
Echoing my letter, lie for lie.
Truth or lies I know not. Which unfaithful,
He or I.

# [I read a statement]

I read a statement in a newspaper
That Twentyman, the manufacturer,
Found it was cheaper to deliver goods
By horse and lorry than by motor-truck
Or motor-van. So he had sold his trucks
To purchase horses. He dismissed those men
Who had mechanics' minds to re-employ
Drivers of horses, friends of animals.
Then life grew stronger in me because life
Had triumphed in this case and would perhaps
Finally triumph over the machine.
Even such mean commercial victory
Being better than no victory at all.


# [I am no mystic. All the ways of God]

I am no mystic. All the ways of God
Are dark to me.
I know not if he lived or if he died
In agony.

My every act has reference to man.
Some human need
Of this one, or of that, or of myself
Inspires the deed.

But when I hear the Angelus, I say
A Latin prayer
Hoping the dim incanted words may shine
Some way, somewhere.

Words and a will may work upon my mind
Till ethics turn
To that transcendent mystic love with which
The Seraphim burn.

# A Prayer to Saint Rosa

When I am so worn out I cannot sleep
And yet I know I have to work next day
Or lose my job, I sometimes have recourse
To one long dead, who listens when I pray.

I ask Saint Rose of Lima for the sleep
She went without, three hundred years ago
When, lying on thorns and heaps of broken sherd,
She talked with God and made a heaven so.

Then speedily that most compassionate Saint
Comes with her gift of deep oblivious hours,
Treasured for centuries in nocturnal space
And heavy with the scent of Lima's flowers.

# Bibliography

*Francis McNamara*
John Meredith, *Frank the Poet: The Life and Works of Francis MacNamara* (Studies in Australian Folklore 1), Red Rooster 1979

*Mary Gilmore*
Mary Gilmore, *Old Days, Old Ways: A Book of Recollections*, Angus & Robertson 1963 (first edn 1934)
W.H. Wilde, *Courage a Grace: A Biography of Dame Mary Gilmore*, Melbourne University Press 1988
W.H. Wilde and T. Inglis Moore (eds), *Letters of Mary Gilmore*, Melbourne University Press 1980

*John Shaw Neilson*
A.R. Chisholm (ed.), *The Poems of Shaw Neilson*, Angus & Robertson 1965, rev. edn 1973
Nancy Keesing (ed.), *The Autobiography of John Shaw Neilson*, National Library of Australia 1978

*Lesbia Harford*
Drusilla Modjeska and Marjorie Pizer (eds), *The Poems of Lesbia Harford*, Sirius 1985

# Index of Titles

    HELL AND AFTER

# Index of First Lines

## Also by Les Murray from Carcanet

# Fyfield*Books*

*Two millennia of essential classics*

The extensive Fyfield*Books* list includes

**Djuna Barnes** *The Book of Repulsive Women and other poems* edited by Rebecca Loncraine

**Elizabeth Barrett Browning** *Selected Poems* edited by Malcolm Hicks

**Charles Baudelaire** *Complete Poems in French and English* translated by Walter Martin

**Thomas Lovell Beddoes** *Death's Jest-Book* edited by Michael Bradshaw

**Aphra Behn** *Selected Poems* edited by Malcolm Hicks

*Border Ballads: A Selection* edited by James Reed

**The Brontë Sisters** *Selected Poems* edited by Stevie Davies

**Sir Thomas Browne** *Selected Writings* edited by Claire Preston

**Lewis Carroll** *Selected Poems* edited by Keith Silver

**Paul Celan** *Collected Prose* translated by Rosmarie Waldrop

**Thomas Chatterton** *Selected Poems* edited by Grevel Lindop

**John Clare** *By Himself* edited by Eric Robinson and David Powell

**Arthur Hugh Clough** *Selected Poems* edited by Shirley Chew

**Samuel Taylor Coleridge** *Selected Poetry* edited by William Empson and David Pirie

**Tristan Corbière** *The Centenary Corbière in French and English* translated by Val Warner

**William Cowper** *Selected Poems* edited by Nick Rhodes

**Gabriele d'Annunzio** *Halcyon* translated by J.G. Nichols

**John Donne** *Selected Letters* edited by P.M. Oliver

**William Dunbar** *Selected Poems* edited by Harriet Harvey Wood

**Anne Finch, Countess of Winchilsea** *Selected Poems* edited by Denys Thompson

**Ford Madox Ford** *Selected Poems* edited by Max Saunders

**John Gay** *Selected Poems* edited by Marcus Walsh

**Oliver Goldsmith** *Selected Writings* edited by John Lucas

**Robert Herrick** *Selected Poems* edited by David Jesson-Dibley

**Victor Hugo** *Selected Poetry in French and English* translated by Steven Monte

**T.E. Hulme** *Selected Writings* edited by Patrick McGuinness

**Leigh Hunt** *Selected Writings* edited by David Jesson Dibley

**Wyndham Lewis** *Collected Poems and Plays* edited by Alan Munton

**Charles Lamb** *Selected Writings* edited by J.E. Morpurgo

**Lucretius** *De Rerum Natura: The Poem on Nature* translated by C.H. Sisson

For more information, including a full list of Fyfield*Books* and a contents list for each title, and details of how to order the books, visit the Carcanet website at www.carcanet.co.uk or email info@carcanet.co.uk